WHAT PEOPLE ARE SAY[...]
HASKELL AND *SUGARCOATED*...

Sugarcoated is an amazing book that gives the feeling of sitting in Angie Haskell's kitchen with a warm cup of tea, allowing safety and permission of humanness along the spiritual journey. As the author shares her own life experiences and her research, readers feel like they are not alone as they learn, walk, and experience the prayer of discernment and conscious choice. Angie identifies the dichotomies of instant gratification and long-term rewards as well as the confinements of shame over authentic freedom. Throughout the book, I pictured two enlightened women having a beautiful discussion of identifying the unspoken thoughts, passions, and behaviors with no judgment, only reverence for honoring experiential wisdom while walking a more authentic and hopeful path with God.

—*Ted Wiard, EdD, LPCC, CGC*
Founder, Golden Willow Retreat
Author, *Witnessing Ted: The Journey to Potential through Grief and Loss*

I've known Angie Haskell as an author and friend for more than a decade now, and she's always been a consistent and thought-provoking voice for women. This new book is open, honest, fun, raw, and emotion filled. *Sugarcoated* doesn't shy away from the topics and hard truths with which women struggle. Angie gets back to the real truth and guides readers down a celebratory path that is uniquely Angie.

—*Dan Lynch*
Brentwood Press

As pastors for over twenty-five years, we have counseled many women regarding temptations and addictions. Angie has not only written a book that accurately identifies the raw struggles women face today, but it offers achievable steps in overcoming them. Using her own vulnerability, she encourages women to draw closer to Christ in their journey. Angie's honesty, sweet personality and Kentucky charm shine throughout this insightful and provoking book. *Sugarcoated* can bust down real walls in a very real way.

—*Bryan and Cindy Hallmark*
Lead pastors, Christian Life Church, Santa Fe, NM

ANGIE HASKELL

SUGAR COATED

FINDING SWEET RELEASE FROM CRAVINGS THAT CONTROL US

WHITAKER
HOUSE

Note: This book is not intended to provide medical advice or to take the place of medical advice and treatment from your personal physician. Neither the publisher nor the author takes any responsibility for any possible consequences from any action taken by any person reading or following the information in this book. Always consult your physician or other qualified health care professional before undertaking any change in your physical regimen, whether fasting, diet, medications, or exercise.

Unless otherwise indicated, all Scripture quotations are taken from the *Holy Bible, New International Version*®, NIV®, © 1973, 1978, 1984, 2011 by Biblica, Inc.® Used by permission of Zondervan. All rights reserved worldwide. www.zondervan.com. The "NIV" and "New International Version" are trademarks registered in the United States Patent and Trademark Office by Biblica, Inc.® Scripture quotations marked (ESV) are taken from *The Holy Bible, English Standard Version*, © 2016, 2001, 2000, 1995 by Crossway Bibles, a division of Good News Publishers. Used by permission. All rights reserved. Scripture quotations marked (NLT) are taken from the *Holy Bible, New Living Translation*, © 1996, 2004, 2015 by Tyndale House Foundation. Used by permission of Tyndale House Publishers, Inc., Carol Stream, Illinois 60188. All rights reserved. Boldface type in the Scripture quotations indicates the author's emphasis.

SUGARCOATED
Finding Sweet Release from Cravings that Control Us

www.angiehaskell.com

ISBN: 979-8-88769-096-4
eBook ISBN: 979-8-88769-097-1

Printed in the United States of America
© 2024 by Angie Haskell

Whitaker House
1030 Hunt Valley Circle
New Kensington, PA 15068
www.whitakerhouse.com

LC record available at https://lccn.loc.gov/2023041538
LC ebook record available at https://lccn.loc.gov/2023041539

1 2 3 4 5 6 7 8 9 10 11 ⨇ 31 30 29 28 27 26 25 24

DEDICATION

To my creative cowboy, William.
Thank you for riding into my life.
Regardless of whether I'm feeling like a woman or
acting like a girl,
you never fail to treat me like a lady.
I love you madly.

CONTENTS

PART ONE

SATISFYING A SWEET TOOTH

Whatever their bodies do affects their souls.
It is funny how mortals always picture us as putting
things into their minds: in reality our best work is done
by keeping things out.
—C. S. Lewis, *The Screwtape Letters*

1

SPINNING OUT OF CONTROL

From the very first time I saw a kid whack one open with a stick, I've been strangely intrigued by piñatas.

Growing up in Kentucky, my only experience with such novelties was seeing them featured in a kid's birthday party scene on TV. I even went so far as to ask Santa for a piñata when I was eight. Unfortunately, the man in the big red suit must have assumed it was too weird a request, as one never found its way under our Christmas tree.

As a former high school history teacher, it was interesting to discover that piñatas were brought to Europe as a result of Marco Polo's travels in China. It would be many years later before Mexico adopted this tradition for which they're more commonly recognized. Perhaps it's just the musings of a twisted author, but there's something surreal about smashing to bits a colorful work of art that took such precious time to create. I'm not ashamed to admit that even a little sadness creeps into my heart when I watch others cheer as a piñata's weak spot is exposed, causing its contents to spill everywhere.

Since raising two daughters in Kentucky, moving to New Mexico, and surviving a divorce that left me emotionally and financially broken, I've seen the similarities between a piñata and my own life. God strangely placed this on my heart when I attended a Hispanic preteen's birthday party. Before the cake was cut, the cracking open of a piñata was part of the children's highly anticipated festivities. I marveled as they cheered for one another, wildly chanting, "Hit it harder! Harder!" Oh, but my mind had wandered off on a parallel that left me speechless and gutted. It was all I could do to sing "Happy Birthday," as God whispered into my ear, *"You're just like that piñata, aren't you, Angie? But dear one, it's okay, I am here. But good grief, let's stop this spinning, shall we?"*

Oh dear. I was busted, pun intended.

Whether it's barely hearing the doctor's words, "I can't promise you'll survive this," filing heart-wrenching divorce papers, or suffering vomit-inducing betrayal by a loved one, I've taken my share of hard knocks. I feel you shaking your head along with me. We've all looked up at God, screaming, feeling totally blindfolded and unable to reach the answers we so desperately seek. In anguish, we resort to swinging at constantly moving targets until we're dizzy and bone-tired from trying so hard.

It is only a matter of time before our hearts are cracked wide open and we grasp at anything remotely palatable to help us avoid pain.

When preparing to write this book, I couldn't help but reflect on my own life and those times I'd subconsciously altered my former refined palate. Oh, I'm not talking about the ability to taste everything from mineral to mocha in a glass of red wine. (Girlfriend, I can barely tell one wine from another.) I'm referring to those times when I moved away from God, forgetting to put my actions through the filter of His Word and instructions.

Since almost all of us have tried one diet or more in our adult life (I fall into the "more" category), I thought it best to compare our struggles to those dangerous sweets that get us into some serious trouble. Oh, we know what puts the pounds on us—coconut cake, pecan pie, chocolate doughnuts, buttery caramels... Okay, I gotta stop here before I make a break for the closest Santa Fe bakery. My point is that we all know what tastes *oh so good* going down comes with a high cost later. Whether it's on the bathroom scale or in our jeans (I could include swimsuits here, but it's just too painful), we get the picture rather quickly that we've indulged in the wrong things.

One way or another, we pay a price for giving in to our cravings.

But the temptations we're going to discuss in this book have far greater consequences than going up a pant size. Although it will be done with love, I'm going to be as honest with you as the number on your scale. We're going to take a hard look at *why* and *what* we reach for to quench our physical and emotional cravings.

In keeping with the above analogy, many of us turn to *candy* or some artificially sweet indulgence as a distraction from reality. Oh, we love having our sweet tooth satisfied, trying to forget the pleasure is far from permanent. But I think we'll agree that there's always more to the story. After all, we exist in a world surrounded by half-truths.

From social media to streaming channels, we are pressured to look like our app-altered photos and taught to believe our marriage should be nothing short of the hottest romance novel, sans the handcuffs or bodice ripping. *Sheesh...* And as a consequence of the pressure to look all put together, we often resort to careless behaviors and half-truths—*anything to avoid facing our own insecurities.*

Whether it's needing that third glass of wine, binge-watching pornography, or engaging in an extramarital affair, our heart races and those feel-good brain receptors make us tingle all over. Trust me, I understand. *But those sensations only last for a while.* Eventually we come to the raw realization that those hard-candy choices weren't nearly as sweet as we'd fantasized. In fact, they were merely wrapped in fake packaging and proved to be tasteless. Before we know it, our body comes down from the rush, and we feel a sense of hollowness unlike anything we've ever experienced. Our conscience embarks on a downward spiral into a sea of shame, so far down that we couldn't care less if oxygen is even offered.

I've had my share of desperation, from self-inflicted wounds that still haunt me today to one incident in which I was totally blindsided, leaving me with big choices to make. Regardless of the situation, one would think a strong Christian woman could have easily battled her way through, clinging to her faith and the constant assurances of His Word.

Hmmm. Not so much.

I've struggled just as you have, often wondering if God thinks this hippie-chick Christian girl is even worth saving. I've stumbled into my bathroom, having had one glass of wine too many, and screamed, "Girl, what has happened to you? *Who are you?!*" Big ugly tears frequently caused mascara to streak down my face. Yet even in the midst of hopelessness, I noticed it was time to color my gray hair, and my muffin-top stomach was spilling over my waistband. Sister, we are our own worst critics, leaving no stone unturned, especially when heaving a boulder at ourselves.

Get ready. Being raw and real is the only way to handle gargantuan temptations and wrestle them to the ground.

But have hope! We *can* and will spare ourselves shame and regret if we patiently learn to fill our minds with healthier options. Perhaps the purging of poisons is overdue for you as well? It is a process that even the most secure of women wouldn't dare to choose unless their very souls depended on it. Perhaps you've felt desperate and disgusted with your decisions, feeling as if your very sanity teetered on the brink of no return. Do you feel as if your countless number of poor choices have deemed you unworthy of other relationships, especially one with Christ?

My sweet friend, nothing could be further from the truth.

How do I know?

I've been there.

As a child, I was taught to fear God more than relish in His grace and mercy. Consequently, I lived much of my early Christian walk waiting for the other shoe to drop with a giant thud. Seeing God as a punisher instead of a pardoner, I was convinced that even the slightest wrong decision would result in harsh consequences.

In talking with women around the country, I find a great majority of them are guilty of this skewed way of thinking. No wonder we struggle to stop our heads from spinning and can barely put one foot in front of the other. When our weak spot is exposed one time too many, we grow sick of indulging and fall to the floor in shame and disgust with ourselves.

And yet for some reason, unbeknownst to our logical brain—which we'll most certainly discuss later—we shake off memories of the negative consequences and fall for the temptations all over again. Positive we're well past the gentle grace period, we hide under our shell of emptiness once more, preparing for the bolt of lightning to strike.

Dear reader, the constant spiraling has got to stop. Let's take off the blindfold, search out our weak spots, and purge the negative habits that rob us of feeling worthy.

May I make an assumption on our behalf? I can't help but think that many of us are white-knuckle terrified that if our candy stash is taken away too quickly, we'll go into withdrawal or even be comatose due to lack of pleasure. *It's okay to admit it.* The process of curbing our cravings and making healthier choices does sound painful. Perhaps we fear life won't be quite as stimulating without that all-too-familiar sugar rush? Oh, sister, if only we could learn from the very first bite that these longings can get us into a whole heap of trouble.

I cannot say this enough: *you're in good company.* I still have empty-wrapper memories of feeling completely broken as a result of my poor choices. The void in my heart was absolutely excruciating. I can sense you have had similar experiences. Your emotional and physical highs have finally exposed themselves as artificially sweet fantasies with a short half-life.

I hope you feel me holding your hand as I say, "It's time to remove the pretty packaging and take a closer look at the ingredients."

This is not an easy conversation. I'm overjoyed that you're taking the first step, as it's most definitely the toughest. Millions of women are sick of being sick, and I'm determined to help us silence the constant whispering of the enemy that lures us down the wrong path. This journey toward well-being requires honesty, courage, and a willingness to admit that some of our choices were completely careless.

It also requires an acceptance that we may stumble and fall more than once along this rocky path. *But you must no longer berate yourself into believing you're past the point of redemption.* You are God's child, period. Will you please reread that? Seriously, go ahead. I'll wait. Whether or not you feel Him at the moment, He is your coach, your encourager, and the one whispering, "Lace up those sneakers, and let's hit the trail."

This book is an attempt to stop you in your tracks at a critical crossroad, where temptations turn into addictions.

I understand if you aren't sure of your exact location on this wobbly footpath. Confusion and, of course, denial, are part of the process. As I said before, I totally get it.

The first seven chapters are written as proof that you're not alone in the struggle. You'll read both painful and uplifting stories of women I met while conducting research for this book. Although their names have been changed, they've been down in the trenches like you. They have prayed for the bombing overhead to stop, but had no idea how to wave the white flag.

You'll also get a glimpse into my own life, including lessons I learned the hard way. If I can help other women stop the madness in their own lives, then it's worth me being raw and real.

The second half of the book will put women's urges and desires under a microscope. Now that we've identified the problem, we need to stop it from reoccurring before it does any more damage.

Girlfriend, you are not alone in this life-altering mission. You have arrived at a safe place among others who have been tempted—*women just like you*—and want to change. Whether you're fiercely hanging on to hidden sins or have bravely chosen to own up to them and seek help, know that Jesus is still madly in love with you.

Let me remind you of Romans 5:8: "*While we were still sinners, Christ died for us.*" *Us* means you and me. Whether you've stopped, are still struggling, or are hiding in shame, God still loves you unconditionally. He wants His children to make choices that bring true fulfillment. This earth or *kitchen* He's created is chock-full of nourishing options. We must simply learn to identify and acquire a taste for that which is good for our mind, body, and spirit.

Right now, you may be sickened with your choices that leave you feeling completely hollow. You're convinced it's only a matter of time before your life falls apart in front of everyone.

Dear one, God is willing and able to pick up the tiny fragments of what seems to be a broken life. He can put you back together.

When I was a teacher, I showed my students how to make a real piñata. Perhaps you've tried it as well? It requires layer upon layer of glue and paper that must become dry and hardened. It takes time to create such a hard, outer shell. Once dry, the piñata is painted and decorated, often garishly, to cover up the multitude of layers of glued paper. The finishing touch is cutting an inconspicuous hole, *a weak spot*, in the piñata and stuffing it with tempting candies. After completing every arduous step, the fun comes in the celebratory process. All cheer as the colorful character is ripped apart, causing its contents to spill onto the ground.

Reread that description.

It is a celebratory process.

While I can't promise every person will cheer as you forge down this path littered with hard candy choices, be rest assured this much-needed cleanse will be a cathartic one. You'll discover what gives you inner peace and learn to let go of those people or habits that rob you of joy. It's time to do this. Let's give God the control, learn how to be properly nourished, and sing together in His kitchen. Will you join me? It takes great courage, but I know you've got the right appetite to make it happen. Hallelujah!

Let's get this party started.

2

A SPOONFUL OF SUGAR

I closed my eyes, praying my credit card would approve of such a grandiose purchase: a designer handbag that was three times the price I'd ever paid for one before. The adrenaline rush was palpable as I watched the salesclerk place the bag in its own cloth pouch and then into a luxurious box. Sweet victory! I strutted out of the store, feeling like Julia Roberts in *Pretty Woman*[1] when she'd confronted the rude boutique employee after shopping at other stores. My reality was not even close. I'd just received a promotion at work and was determined to flex my independence...or in this case, my credit card. Surely I'd feel better then.

But before I'd even exited the mall, an avalanche of uncertainty began to form in the pit of my stomach. *What had I just done?* With sweaty palms, I unlocked my car door, ducked inside to escape the freezing rain, looked into the rearview mirror, and sobbed. As a mom with two young daughters, I began to

---

1. *Pretty Woman*, directed by Garry Marshall (1990; Buena Vista Pictures Distribution).

question my sanity for making such an irresponsible purchase. And to make matters worse, I soon felt worthless once again. My vain attempt to feel good, to feel anything, took place over twenty-five years ago, and I still struggle on occasion. Regardless of the timeline, there was one thing I was sure of: Mary Poppins lied to me.

Sugar did not help the medicine go down.

The children in this Disney classic[2] learned to carry out unpleasant chores with the help of a little candy. Just a taste of sweetness from their wise nanny seemed to change their perspective in a New York minute. When I was a stressed-out mom, I totally related to this fictional character. I bribed my children with candy more than once. Oh, the organizers of store checkout lines are masters in the art of temptation. They know we'll grab the first sugar-laden treat in sight if it will stop our kids from screaming.

When desperation takes hold of us, we'll do anything to get a little peace, even if it's temporary.

As I sat in my car wondering how I'd pay my ever-increasing credit card bill, I came to a distinct realization: my little designer handbag did not make my emotional pain easier to accept. Not in the least. However, it was an easy fix that had become familiar. Throughout adulthood, anytime I'd ever felt sad, lonely, or undesirable, I'd always turned to shopping to soothe my insecurities. Whether purchasing cosmetics, shoes, handbags, or clothes, it was my go-to, my quick fix to feel better. Part of it

---

2. *Mary Poppins*, directed by Robert Stevenson (1964; Walt Disney Productions).

was learned behavior from observing close family members who struggled with their own insecurities. But excuses aside, I had to own up to my actions and come clean: I was not merely tempted by certain *sweets*, I'd become addicted. My costly treat was merely disguised in different packaging.

Perhaps you can relate.

When life's disappointments occur, many women develop a litany of insecurities and wrestle with them for years. Feeling undesirable after an affair, worthless due to endless criticism by a parent, or yearning to feel needed after our children couldn't help but grow up, life's gut punches put us on the floor. We think twice before getting back on our feet. In our emptiness, we develop cravings; we are tempted to do whatever it takes to feel passion, to feel desirable, to be relieved of pain.

These urges manifest themselves like a box of assorted chocolates, always leaving us longing for more.

Compulsive shopping, binge-watching pornography, substance abuse, marital affairs, and obsessions with our physical appearance are some of the raw topics we'll discuss in this book. Just know, my friend, that it will be done with love and empathy.

But be forewarned, there is one common denominator amidst all of these behaviors: *they're often in disguise, and they're always dangerous.* Sure, the shiny packaging will lure you in. You'll feel exhilarated and perhaps feel a quick physical high. But just as quickly as you feel the jolt of temporary pleasure, you'll be sick with regret. The vicious cycle can spin wilder than a Texas tornado as you crave, feel sick over your actions, and then crave again. That's how the enemy works. After surrendering to personal urges, we are always left unfulfilled and yearning for more. And since most of us women are impatient—we might as well admit it!—we settle for the quick fix to satiate our craving.

The euphoria associated with my handbag purchase didn't last past the parking lot. Still, I continued to shop in order to feel good about myself. Why didn't I learn my lesson after that first spontaneous splurge that seriously damaged my bank account? Why can't a binge eater stop eating an entire chocolate cake, even though they're aware of the extra pounds and health consequences? Why do women spend hours of their day binge-watching a racy TV series, while ignoring the greater responsibilities of real relationships?

We beg God to help us resist temptation and get angry if He doesn't do it our way. We even go so far as to blame Him for allowing us to get so hungry in the first place, especially if our cravings turn into full-fledged addictions. Oh, how we love to argue with our heavenly Father.

Why is it so darn difficult to resist temptation?

In conducting research for this section, my first interview subject was my youngest daughter, Channing. Not only was she the illustrator of my first middle grade book series, *The Desperate Diva Diaries*, she grew up to become a brilliant cognitive psychologist. I have no doubt God knew I'd need all the help I could muster in understanding my little brain. Ladies, don't shoot the messenger, but we need to do a scientific deep dive to gain better insight into what's going on in our heads.

I'll make it as brief and painless as possible.

In addition to knowing that we live in a fallen world, the cyclical struggle with temptation is related to how one's brain is wired and a chemical called dopamine. Although the brain contains many types of neurotransmitters—those chemicals that transmit information between neurons—dopamine regulates our learning and emotional responses. Known as the *feel good* receptor, it also enables one to not only visualize rewards, but also take action and move toward them. Since dopamine contributes to feelings of pleasure and satisfaction as part of the reward system, the neurotransmitter plays a critical role in cravings, temptations, and addictions.

Let's take a neurological look at ourselves for a few paragraphs.

According to neurologists and psychologists, when we take steps to do something enjoyable, dopamine is naturally released into the brain area called the nucleus accumbens (NAc). This section, which is located near the center of the brain, inherently associates the release of dopamine with a euphoric, rewarding sensation.

For this reason, the NAc is often called the brain's *pleasure center*. However, its responsiveness can have very unpleasant consequences. Research shows that substance abuse and other addictive behaviors are also directly linked to the NAc. While abused substances have their own pharmacological effect, continued use causes the brain to quickly identify them with a rewarding release of dopamine.

Over time and with continued use of the *candy* of our choosing, the brain continues to release more and more dopamine into the NAc. This means that the more we indulge and try to satisfy our perceived craving, the more the brain associates it with pleasure. Once we understand the incredibly strong effect this can have on our physical sensations and emotions, destructive behavior is easier to understand.

But the plot thickens here. The dopamine release associated with addiction is not limited to illicit substances. In fact, when *any* activity or substance is continually associated with satisfaction, dopamine is released into the brain. These activities may not be rewarding ones, but *our brain tricks us and makes us think they are.* Unfortunately, this means that any number of self-destructive behaviors, such as excessive shopping, excessive exercise, or overeating, can cause the brain to develop addictive tendencies.

For example, take my earlier admission of excessive shopping. I see the handbag in the store, and consciously or not, I think of the actress I saw carrying it on the red carpet. I think of her beauty, her seemingly perfect figure, and the nonstop camera flashes that reassure her of just how great she is. I take the handbag off the shelf, hang it on my shoulder, and imagine what all of my girlfriends will think when they see it on my arm. Maybe they'll think I'm beautiful too. Maybe they'll think I'm successful. I might not even be thinking these things consciously; they could just be whispers in the back of my mind. But before I know it, I'm at the sales counter and then sitting in my car, wondering how exactly I'd talked myself into another purchase.

By continuing to imagine satisfaction and the approval of friends, I begin to convince myself that the act of shopping is rewarding, satisfying, and helping me to achieve my (unachievable) goal. By imagining these results over and over, the prospective satisfaction becomes tied to the act of shopping itself, causing my brain to release a crazy amount of dopamine.

Unfortunately, no one ever warned me how easy it is to hijack a God-given brain system. Designed to experience joy, accomplish dreams, and reach well-intended goals, our brain gets kidnapped by toxic individuals who prefer to belittle and question our need for respect. Through fear and intimidation, we are subconsciously led down a path just far enough to get lost. It's incredible how the enemy works, using the very nature of our bodies, our weak flesh, to harm us.

Girlfriend, I can't say enough how much I understand what you're going through. It takes courage to own up to unhealthy cravings, to acknowledge one's *secret candy stash* and even end relationships that threaten our sanity. It takes even greater strength to *change* those habits and put an end to the consumption of sweets that suck the ever-livin' life from us. Sure, you'll most likely have setbacks, but with God's help, your brain and heart will make a strong connection. It is my prayer that after reading this book, you'll be a superhero in resisting temptation. *Again, be patient with yourself.*

I'd love to tell you that I no longer resort to shopping for a dopamine rush, but I promised to be honest with you, so I have to admit I'm still a work in progress. While we can only take responsibility for ourselves, we must remove our rosy sunglasses and acknowledge the painful situations staring back at us.

While some hardships are out of our control, they can foster a yearning to escape or cave in to a temptation. If there's one life struggle, there's a hundred. Aging parents, divorce, worries with adult children or grandchildren, personal health scares, and economic nightmares can dash retirement hopes and dreams. From my bathroom floor, I've looked toward heaven on more than one occasion, screaming, "I'm *so* sick and tired of this roller coaster, God. I'm ready to cash in my tickets and just walk away."

You may have uttered such frustration yourself. If so, you're in good company. In conducting research for this book, hundreds of women recalled having similar conversations with God. They questioned Him after being beaten by their husbands. After being with a lover, they screamed at God on the drive home, rattled with guilt. They yelled at God while drunk, as their grief was too much to bear. They shouted at God after checking their kid into rehab for the second time, all while having their third drink of scotch. *We all have screamed at God when experiencing pain.* We all have pleaded for strength and understanding. We beg God to help us resist temptation and get angry if He doesn't do it our way. Thankfully, we have a Holy Spirit who can speak calm into us.

It may require you to be quiet and still for a while, but if you listen, you will hear.

No? I've never been a good listener either.

A few years ago, I took on a role that I'd daydreamed about for years: *empty nester.* Although I'd cherished (almost!) every day of being a mother to two daughters, I envisioned seeing them off to college with great jubilation. There were days I was positive the roof might cave in. By the time your angels are eighteen, they're ready to use their little wings and fly. (We'll talk more about that in an upcoming chapter.) I polished their halos and sent them on their way.

Although I was still working, retirement was only a few years away. Visions of traveling, trying out new hobbies, doing *whatever* and *whenever* was the ultimate goal. I counted down each day like an advent calendar, anticipating a surprise behind every door. In only a few years, my life was going to be like one of those pharmaceutical ads featuring retirees cruising around the country in a motorhome. I could hardly wait to throw caution to the wind and live life with reckless abandon.

Let's just say that dream didn't quite work out as planned.

Not even close.

Three months after my oldest daughter went away to college and right after I'd received a nice financial bonus, I was rear-ended by a semitruck. Suddenly, the job I loved and from which I'd planned to retire ended with a loud, literal crash. I was left with crippling anxiety and a debilitating neurological condition called chronic regional pain syndrome (CRPS). The pain in my neck, shoulder, and right arm was so horrendous, I wondered if suicide might be a better option than living. Aside from a spinal cord stimulator, no surgeon was willing to operate for fear the condition could worsen. In a single moment, my life turned totally upside down. My dream of retiring with security had become a nightmare saddled with uncertainty.

I was in no mood to sit quietly and hope to hear from the Holy Spirit. I preferred to lie on a sofa and feel sorry for myself. Not only did I become angry at God, but I felt like a useless human being. My kids no longer needed me as much, my career had tragically come to an end, and I saw myself as a total failure. My world was filled with anger, rage, depression, anxiety, and— you guessed it—temptations and cravings.

Not only did my career end, but my self-worth dwindled to microscopic levels. To make matters worse, my husband began to work longer night shift hours while yours truly craved emotional and physical intimacy more than ever. The lack of it became the eight-hundred-pound gorilla who refused to budge. My desire to ride off into the sunset had gone dark and cold. I preferred to get angry, fall victim to temptations, and plot ways to attain immediate satisfaction. Since you're now knowledgeable about the brain and its use of dopamine, I'm sure you can guess which *fake sweet* I reached for the most.

That's right. *Shopping.*

Whether it was a new sweater I didn't need or a pair of heels I'd never wear, the UPS guy came to my house on a regular basis. I no longer had a job and didn't need these things in the least, but still, I shopped. My husband was ready to bribe the delivery guy to stay out of our driveway. Have mercy.

But thanks to doctors who insisted I see a therapist specializing in pain and job loss, I had no choice but to take a deeper look at my actions. They were contributing to my pain and causing serious difficulties in a marriage that was already struggling. I had to surrender my insecurities to God and realize I was loved and valued, regardless of whether I had a job outside the home. I equated having a successful, high-paying career with value… but God didn't.

Have you ever been guilty of putting reputation and appearances above reality? Sweet friend, our brains can certainly get their wires crossed. And like an evil puppeteer who thrives on knotting things up, the enemy loves it.

Regardless of our circumstances, it's time we learn to accept God's medicine, which is far different than the bribery Mary Poppins used to coax the children into line. I'm talking about that which God gives us freely and abundantly—that jaw-dropping thing called grace. We must also commit to better understanding His Word, to seek help from professionals when needed, and be willing to consider medication, if deemed necessary and prescribed by a doctor. Dear friend, we must be willing to do whatever is necessary to get mentally healthy as God untangles the mess we've gotten ourselves into. We'll talk more about this in upcoming chapters.

Since being forthright is crucial, we need to remember that while we still wrestle with old cravings, new ones can develop over time. The deep desires of a fifty-six-year-old female will be quite different than that of a thirty-five-year-old mom with young kids at home. Each new stage of life brings its own fair share of joy, heartache, and confusion, and new temptations to go along with those.

Why do I get the feeling you're in the middle of your own gut-wrenching roller coaster ride? I'm right here with you, friend. Let's pop an antacid together. Together we are going to stop the madness. By remembering temptations will always be a part of our lives here on earth, we must grow stronger in God's Word. We must emotionally prepare ourselves for what might be lurking around the corner. *Detoxing ourselves from harmful temptations takes time.*

When the enemy knows our weakness, he doesn't stop after one attempt. Instead, he tries to make our life repeat itself, going 'round and 'round. And just like a worn-out Eagles record played one too many times, when the scratches are ignored, the music eventually comes to a screeching halt. If you picked up this book to stop the spinning, to arm yourself with knowledge and preparedness, then *you* deserve an enormous hug. You're a step ahead of so many others who are hurting.

Whether you're tempted to engage in inappropriate relationships, use drugs, or watch pornography, or even have the constant need to feel beautiful, we're going to have a heart to heart, sister to sister, and face all of our temptations with love and compassion.

Are you ready?

As for this anxiety-ridden Southern girl who used to hide candy wrappers...er, shopping receipts, God is empowering me with strength I never knew I had or deserved. Through prayer and therapy, I'm learning to face my fears, close my eyes to cravings, and realize I was created to accomplish great things in this life.

So are you. God loves you to pieces and wants you to be your authentic self. He accepts you with open arms, whether your hands are sticky from sweet cravings, you're wearing leopard high heels that you really didn't need, or something else entirely.

With strength from a compassionate Savior, we'll learn to develop healthy cravings that have nothing to do with sugar. Not even a spoonful.

Take *that*, Mary Poppins!

3

SUGARCOATING IT

September 11, 2001. The space shuttle explosion. The death of Michael Jackson. The death of Prince. *I love music, what can I say?* There are days we remember exactly what we were doing when the tragic news broke.

August 31, 1997, is another date seared into my brain. I'd turned on the television while helping my six-year-old daughter pick up her mess of a bedroom. From Barbie shoes to Polly Pocket pieces, it was a health risk to enter my sweet girl's room with bare feet, risking impalement by a plastic accessory. I'd been too physically exhausted to attempt to clear the disaster area the night before. As a working mom determined to prove *women can have it all*, my nerves were shot most of the time.

Now Tom Brokaw's words had forced me to sit on my child's bed and cry quietly, trying not to scare my six-year-old. The people's princess had died while we Americans were slumbering. The news stations switched between showing the mangled limousine in Paris to photos of Diana's glamorous life and her adorable sons. I switched stations and listened to the news anchors on every channel and still couldn't believe what I'd just heard. Like millions of other women, I'd been an admirer of the Princess of Wales for years. She seemed to have the total package: elegance, wealth, a beautiful family, and the ability to help social issues close to her heart. But now, all I could think about were two little boys in London who had just lost their mummy. As I looked at my innocent daughter who asked why I was crying, I mentally told myself to cherish every single second. Picking up Barbie shoes had suddenly become a small blessing.

Over the following days of news coverage, every journalist seemed to enjoy pointing out Princess Diana's personal problems: her divorce from Prince Charles, her bouts of anxiety and depression, and her struggle with bulimia. These, along with her alleged affairs, were issues constantly heard over the airwaves. The media never knows when to stop. Ironically, I'd never heard about Diana's struggles with bulimia until after her death. If it had been public knowledge previously, perhaps I chose not to listen. I was shocked and dumbfounded when they replayed the infamous interview of her recounting the numerous times she'd locked herself in the bathroom and forced herself to vomit.

My mind kept asking itself the same question: *Why on earth would a woman so gorgeous and admired, a princess loved by the world, willingly force herself to throw up? Why?*

Perhaps her cravings led her to make some very inappropriate decisions—*choosing the wrong candy*—like the rest of us? Perhaps you can relate? I'm convinced that when the tiara and makeup came off each night, Diana was just like most women: exhausted, in need of compassion, and craving love, all while worrying if her beauty was slowly fading. God rest her soul, it was almost as if one could see the pain in those incredible blue eyes.

Sadly, she chose to sugarcoat her reality, a bleak existence that was a far cry from what her admirers envisioned. Although Diana was stunningly beautiful, had two healthy sons, and had her choice of designer clothes and jewelry, it was still not enough. Her cravings led to a restless soul and unsteady thoughts that resulted in bulimia, inappropriate relationships, and scrutiny by the entire world.

Diana chose to cover up her body insecurities and her deeper emotional struggles by purging food. It was her way of trying to force the emotional pain out of her body. Coming from an aristocratic family, Lady Diana Frances Spencer lived a privileged life. Her family lineage included Winston Churchill. When she was eight, she and her siblings were engulfed in a nasty custody battle; as a result, they were primarily raised by their father. Unhappy living with her father and his second wife, Diana struggled as a teen. She failed in school repeatedly and eventually dropped out at age sixteen. When she met Charles, he was actually already dating her older sister and then Camilla Shand (Parker Bowles).

What a troublesome life Diana had, even before acquiring the title Princess of Wales. I'll always wonder if it was a specific event or life in general that led her to kneeling in front of the toilet, sticking her finger down her throat, and forcing up what was probably a delicious meal served on the world's finest china. God bless this beloved woman who'd experienced such pain.

Although I've never chosen to rid myself of food through bulimia, I can understand why women do it: *anything to achieve temporary control over a life that seems hopeless.* Sweet friend, if you suffer from any type of eating disorder or have found yourself on a diet for as long as you can remember, know there are compassionate physicians and counselors to help you. You are a beautiful child of God and may need a little assistance in being reminded of that glorious fact. *But for now, just remember you are loved.* We'll tackle these cravings more seriously in the second half of this book. I promise.

Unfortunately, I don't know a single female who hasn't indulged in the wrong kind of *candy,* hoping to rid herself of emotional distress, extra pounds, or wrinkles. There's not enough ink to list all of the unfair flaws that we see in the mirror. It's heartbreaking that we're so stinking hard on ourselves. We're way past due to slow down, put on our eyeglasses (some of us are just now admitting we need them), and take a closer look at ourselves.

It's time.

One of the biggest issues with which many of us struggle is poor body image, just as Princess Diana did. It leads many to overeat out of frustration, starve ourselves out of hopelessness, or regurgitate food out of shame and fear over what we've eaten. And make no mistake, it starts at a very young age. The 2015 Common Sense Media Research Study[3] provides some staggering statistics:

+ 80 percent of ten-year-old girls have been on a diet. In 1970, the average dieting age was fourteen.

+ More than half of girls and one-third of boys ages six to eight want thinner bodies.

3. "Children, Teens, Media, and Body Image," *Common Sense Media,* 2015, www.commonsensemedia.org/research.

✦ It is estimated that almost 1.3 million adolescent girls in the United States have anorexia.

The data is heartbreaking.

Many studies conclude that the average woman is on a diet for thirty-one years over the course of her life. *Thirty-one years!* For over three decades of our lives, most of us have been on a gazillion diets—protein, paleo, high fat, low fat, keto, vegan, Mediterranean, French, all fruit, all veggies, all soup, all liquid, raw food… You name it. Good gracious, it's no wonder we feel so exhausted and emotionally wrecked.

Of course, we don't dare let anyone *know* of our frailties, since the walls of social media must look perfectly painted. Appearances matter more than ever, or at least that's what we tell ourselves. Whether it's abusing our bodies into starvation, altering ourselves past recognition with cosmetic fillers, or sugarcoating our selfies using the latest phone app, we indulge in every kind of imaginable *candy*—all due to insecurity and cravings.

The first time I heard the song "Sugar Coat"[4] by Little Big Town on the radio, I had to pull my car off of the road and sob. I'd never heard a woman sing words so profound, as if she'd secretly been hiding out in my closet or under my bed. It reiterates what we women know already: the pressure to look like we have the perfect life, regardless of whether we're ready to crack on the inside, is enormous. As lamented in the song, when faced with insurmountable pressure, many women are tempted to throw caution to the wind and break free. However, out of fear of retribution, we jerk on our *sugar coat*, paste on a whitened

---

4. Little Big Town, "Sugar Coat," on *Nightfall* (Capitol Nashville, 2019).

smile, and make sure our social media posts are nothing short of perfection.

Mercy.

Regardless of why we're wearing it or for whom, we must free ourselves of this sugar coat before it rots our self-worth to the core. I know, girlfriend, it's hard to remove, especially since it was probably handed down from another woman in your life who insisted you be a nice girl and wear it.

No more. We're going to burn these fake fashions in the fire together.

But before unfastening that first rhinestone button, let's own up to another related pressure. It's but one more stressor trying to convince us that our exterior should sparkle more than the crystal gathering dust in our china cabinet.

At some point in our adult lives, most of us have yearned to look sexy and desirable for someone. *Finally, the secret is out.* It's not like any of us didn't know this already. We're surrounded by it and have been our entire lives. Yours truly is so guilty, it's almost comical.

In 1980, a hair product was launched that was all the rage. With only a few sprays of this miraculous *sun-infused* product, the company promised one's hair would be covered in gorgeous blonde highlights. People would mistake the user for the very sexy Farrah Fawcett, whose image was plastered on the bedroom wall of every teenage guy. Ugh. But millions of girls like me fell for this miracle product. As a teen with knock-knees and braces, I desperately hoped it would help me feel pretty.

Of course, they failed to mention it *might* not work well on brunettes. It *might* not have enough peroxide in it to really turn one's hair blonde. It *might* make one's hair look and feel like orange shredded wheat. Forget about looking like one of Charlie's Angels.[5] I did, however, look like Bozo the Clown's younger sister. Good gracious. My hair was a mess. And trying to remedy it with a hair product from a pharmacy only made it worse, if such a thing was possible. Between lemon juice, bleach, and $2.99 hair color, it's an ever-loving miracle that I have a hair left on my head. Thank You, merciful Jesus. It's amazing how quickly companies take hold of our insecurities, causing us to fall victim to temptations.

It didn't get easier during my senior year. As a seventeen-year-old, I was bullied in school and struggled with self-confidence. I also suffered from terrible cystic acne. I remember being called *Pizza Face* at my school locker on several occasions. Girls can be downright mean, but I have a feeling you already know that. Those early experiences affect every part of our being. I dated guys who devalued me because that's all I thought I deserved. It's taken years of therapy, reassurance from friends, and reminders from God's Word to constantly jog my brain's twisted memory. I have to look into the mirror and remind myself daily that I am valued and desired by Jesus. That is enough.

I hope you will look into your own mirror and realize that you too are valued and desired by Jesus.

While many women deny they'd ever succumb to such vanity, one only need look at the amount of money spent on

5. *Charlie's Angels*. Created by Ivan Goff and Ben Roberts. ABC, September 22, 1976 – June 24, 1981.

cosmetics, lingerie, workout wear, high heels, and facial fillers. Whether it's purchasing a lacy bra or flavored lip gloss, we shop for many items because they make us feel sexy, thin, or beautiful. Moreover, we yearn for our spouse or significant other to see us the same way.

Of course, women also make clothing, hair, and jewelry choices to get the attention of other women. This has nothing to do with homosexuality and everything to do with our insecurities and the craving to be valued and respected by the women we admire. Women's magazines have made millions of dollars because of this for over a hundred years. We get our fashion inspirations, not to mention tons of advice, from other women—*women who are often just as insecure as we are.*

Add to it the countless hours we spend engaging with social media, and it is only natural that we are tempted to do whatever we deem necessary to look like an airbrushed beauty. Let's be clear: there's nothing dirty or wrong with the desire to look sexy for our spouses. It's when women take it to the extreme, due to deep insecurity, that negative consequences occur. From wearing revealing clothing to overindulging in cosmetic procedures, we can do this *sexy and desirable* thing to our detriment.

While conducting research for this book, I interviewed hundreds of courageous women who were willing to share their stories of struggle. Perhaps there's a glimpse of you hidden somewhere among them.

MELANIE'S STORY

Melanie, age fifty-three, always felt depressed after looking at the glamourous women on social media. They all looked so perfect. Sculpted bodies, sculpted facial features, sculpted everything. One day, after analyzing herself in the mirror, she decided she needed to lose a few pounds. Determined to look more toned, she signed up for a membership at the local gym. Soon, Melanie found herself losing weight and started to go to the gym twice a day. She also began paying more attention to online before and after photos of women who'd had cosmetic procedures. After losing more weight, Melanie began to get facial fillers and other alterations. She saw results and loved how she felt about herself, no matter that it had drained her bank account. Melanie especially loved the comments she received from friends on social media. Her husband grew concerned when their teenage daughter asked if she could get breast implants, insisting she should be able to alter a few things on her body as her mom had done. A few weeks later, Melanie discovered that her daughter had been secretly purging food in the toilet. Suddenly, life seemed out of control.

Sugarcoating ourselves to look perfect is not unusual today. Many are determined to convince themselves—and others—that they have the perfect house, perfect marriage, and perfect children. While we'll be discussing insecurity in greater depth later, we must learn to recognize the enemy's favorite pickup lines: *You're not good enough. You're not pretty enough. You're not getting enough attention.*

Those are lies. All lies.

Insecurity is a big hairy monster that must be confronted and locked up for good. While I know you're shaking your head, saying, "Preach on, Angie," I also realize you completely understand that the big hairy monster has a skeleton key. He has more than one way to bust out and get into your brain. Sadly, this monster can also attack other victims who may be living under your roof.

Our daughters and sons watch our every move and can make our struggles their own.

If we never feel good enough, skinny enough, or perfect enough, there's a really good chance our children will become adults who feel the exact same way. Reread this, my friend. Reread it until it sinks deep into your bones. It's one more reason to dare this insecurity monster to put a single finger on the doorknob. Let's keep the door locked, throw away the key, and limp into the bright light together.

You deserve the spotlight for your willingness to be real.

You don't have to look like a perfect princess to be reminded that you're loved by a King. Be yourself and smile, my friend. You are a child of the Most High. Now, go wear your crown proudly.

It's okay if it's tarnished a bit.

4

SWEET ESCAPES

Although it's been years since that infamous bath soap commercial first aired, I still find myself asking the bubbles to "take me away" while relaxing in the bathtub. I can't help but think that other women still remember that tagline because it so greatly resonated with our needs. Count me in. The most relaxing part of my day has always been enjoying a long hot bath. Sometimes I go so far as to light a lavender candle while clearing my mind amidst the bubbles.

While I've never found statistics to prove it, I'm sure one's blood pressure goes down a few points when soaking their weary bones. It's pure bliss when I climb into the bed with clean skin and then listen to my sound machine emulate a soft rain. Ah, perhaps my diastolic pressure is falling as I write.

With work stress, financial pressures, family issues, and the increasing divide that exists in this country, is it any wonder we yearn to escape from reality? And when we get older and life's challenges grow more serious, so does our craving for a stronger means of escape. For many women, a long bath isn't quite enough. Alcohol, inappropriate relationships, and substance abuse become the *escape candies* of choice. Even busyness is a temptation that can manifest itself at harmful levels, especially if one is an empty nester. I interviewed countless women who confessed that they indulged in one or more harmful habits to avoid confronting the real contributor to their depression. Might I also point out that it's at this stage of life that the divorce rate climbs.

I was one of those women who ignored the elephant until it was about to shove me into a canyon.

The same month that my youngest daughter went away to college, my husband took a new job, and we moved from Kentucky to New Mexico. *The. Same. Month.* I'd lived in Kentucky for over forty-five years and yet I agreed to relocate within days of becoming an empty nester. I still have trouble believing I survived it. Not only was I moving away from my parents, my daughters were attending different colleges in the East, and my closest family member was dying from ovarian cancer.

Carolyn was closer than a sister; she had been my beloved art teacher in high school and knew my insecurities better than anyone. Not only did she understand my fears, Carolyn was well aware of my dreams, especially my longing to live in the Southwest like so many artists before me. When I expressed my concern over the poor timing of my move, she touched my shoulder with her weak right hand and said, "Angie, it's time. You're an artist who needs to find herself. Now go…"

So I went.

But it wasn't long before the newness of our adobe wore off, my marriage became fractured, and I felt there wasn't a single soul alive who needed me. *Friend, I was a mess.* With the exception of our ragdoll cat—who knew where the food was, but was just too lazy to get it—I was positive that if I drove off into the sunset, not a single person would notice. Perhaps you've been there as well.

After a few months of feeling sorry for myself, I decided to pull on my cowgirl boots and try to make a few friends. I was overjoyed to discover that one of the local art museums needed volunteers, especially a former teacher like myself. *They needed me!* Within a few weeks, I was recounting the history of the Santa Fe Trail, pointing out the beauty of Native American rugs, and showing visitors the many types of turquoise found in the Southwest. My calendar filled up so quickly that I had a constant migraine. The word *no* was not in my vocabulary.

After volunteering myself into oblivion, my emotionally regulated pain disorder flared up bigger than ever. My body held up a "Help me" poster that could no longer be ignored. I also had to confront the massive pain in my heart: I missed my daughters who were a thousand miles away, my parents needed me quicker than I could get there, and my lifelong sister in Christ was dying. It was only after Carolyn's passing, and my suffering anxiety and depression, that I sought help from a licensed therapist. He told me that there are other forms of grief besides those associated with death. Grief can be associated with moving from one's home, job loss, and even becoming an empty nester. So I was grieving in some very big ways. While most women usually space such events apart a few years, yours truly used the *go big or go home* tactic to her detriment. I had no choice but to use the wounds I'd suffered and turn them into big ol' scars of wisdom.

Dr. Ted Wiard, a licensed clinical therapist and certified grief counselor in New Mexico, is renowned for his research on grief. He shared with me the reason why there's so much pain associated with loss:

> We live with a high-level illusion of safety. It's how we function. Once we realize we don't have control over a situation, we naturally have discomfort. When we get yanked out of our status quo, or homeostasis, our brain says, "Everything is wrong." So, the grief and anguish are there because we crave how life used to be. Even if that past wasn't perfect, our brain craves homeostasis. When we can't have that, we start to grasp at anything, even if they're unhealthy, to try and create that balance or familiarity.

Eventually, I realized that I had zero control over certain situations. I couldn't stop my kids from growing up and becoming successful, independent adults. I couldn't control the semitruck that hit me, causing me to lose my job. And I couldn't cure Carolyn's cancer, regardless of how hard I prayed. I was powerless. Just as Dr. Wiard said, I grasped at anything, trying to regain that status quo or homeostasis that I craved. Regardless of my escape candy of choice, I always ended up feeling lost, angry, and scared. Why? Because I hadn't yet learned how to cope with my new normal.

How about you? Have you grieved due to uncontrollable situations in your life?

Your marriage looks good on the outside, yet you can't get your husband's affair out of your mind. Your son is addicted to drugs, and he's repeatedly stolen money from your wallet. You raised your daughter in the church, yet you hear of her exploits online that are far removed from her faith. Your husband passed away unexpectedly, and you feel helpless, unsure of where to turn, where to live, or what to do next. Regardless of the source of your pain, it is excruciating. You feel hollow, gutted, and barely able to breathe. It's a chore to even put one foot in front of the other. In such dire situations, it's as if God has left the building. You're positive you heard Him say, "You're on your own, kid. I'm kinda done here."

That's exactly what happened with the Israelites.

God used Moses to lead them out of Egypt to Canaan, *the promised land*. But rather than the quickest route that made the most sense, God led them into the wilderness—hot, dry, barren wasteland, with the Red Sea looming off in the distance. I can almost hear their grumblings, can't you? Where was this *"land flowing with milk and honey"* (Exodus 13:5) they'd heard all about? Although they felt angry and clueless, God had a plan. *He was protecting them.*

To reach Canaan, they would have to fight the Moabites, the Amalekites, and several other nations before actually having to confront the cities and tribes of Canaan itself. The Israelites were in no condition to undertake such a challenge.

God also wanted to teach the Israelites to rely on Him. When they said they were hungry and thirsty, He fed them and gave them water. When the pharaoh's army was on their heels, God parted the Red Sea, allowing Moses to lead His people to safety. *God was there at every step, preparing His children, even when they didn't feel it.*

And just like us, they struggled with their faith.

They still didn't believe God was their watchful Father. Fed up with waiting, they began worshipping a golden calf and old gods they'd had in Egypt. Sadly, it was their way of telling God they were fed up, beat down, and tired of the desert. Sound familiar?

You may also remember what happened after the Israelites' impatient meltdown. *They wandered in the desert for forty years.* They failed to trust their supernatural Father when they could have enjoyed His supernatural blessings. My friend, let that sink in.

Too often, we view the wilderness as a form of punishment. For sure, it can be that place, as it was with the Israelites who caved in to temptation and endured painful consequences. But rather than feeling punished, use your time in the desert to get to know Jesus. Be still and quiet. Prepare your heart for a life filled with incredible blessings.

There's another type of escape candy that must be addressed in this chapter. Friend, I have wrestled with it and talked to God about it, yet repeatedly, I've heard the Holy Spirit whisper that it must be brought into the light. This urge rises from the fullness of a mother's heart; it can leave her feeling completely gutted if not understood. This temptation has little to do with shopping or the desire to look sexy. It has everything to do with the desire to control.

Rather than confront the reality that our role as a parent has somewhat diminished, many women are tempted to over-interfere as a means of staying in the forefront of their adult children's lives. Please forgive me if I'm stepping on your manicured toes, for I am writing this out of compassion and as a woman who's been there. It's also a temptation that's greatly on the rise.

While we've long been preparing for our little birds to soar into adulthood, many women panic when the day finally arrives. It's only natural. We still have emotional bumps and bruises from our own journey. We've been stung by bosses and betrayed by coworkers. We've been slammed with medical bills and slapped with speeding tickets. It only makes sense that we worry, praying our parenting skills have prepared them to be grown-ups. We pray they find a job. We pray they find a soul mate. We pray for their health, and we pray for their happiness.

Yet many mothers are convinced that their adult kids need their supervision more than ever. Teaching children how to tie their shoes, moms often tell themselves, pales in comparison to the skills needed to balance a checkbook, find a place to live, or buy a car. Our kids need our two cents in all of these important matters.

Er, not so much.

When we combine our wisdom with the urge to protect, we cave in to a temptation that can cause harm for years to come. While it may initially feel good to feel needed, it can become a financial or emotional burden that leads to depression, anxiety, or conflict.

I spoke with women who literally followed their kids to college, preventing them from learning to trust their own instincts or enjoy formative years with lifelong friends. Some mothers admitted to almost going bankrupt as a result of paying their kids' bills rather than insisting they get jobs and do it for themselves. One mother informed me that when her husband filed for divorce, he said her inability to stand up to their adult daughter had fractured their marriage beyond repair.

This type of temptation is no different than other struggles with roots of insecurity. Some mothers fear their children won't love them if they don't provide for all their needs. They forget that their son is no longer three, but instead twenty-three. Rather than face rejection or allow their son or daughter to take on more responsibility, a parent may cave in to fear. The mere thought of a child not loving them seems too painful to bear.

Excuse me for being blunt, but if this hits a nerve, perhaps you're not giving your children enough credit. I'd wager the contents of my handbag that you raised your child with immense love, providing them lasting childhood memories. Don't cheapen your child-rearing practices by believing they'll stop loving you unless you give them what they want. *You know better.*

As parents, it our responsibility to prepare our children to soar on their own in a timely fashion. That's our job, not keeping them in the nest until they've weighed it down, threatening the very happiness of the people who built it. You may have sleepless nights or a few days of silence, but some conversations may require you to say, "I love you, but this is your responsibility," or, "You'll need to save up for that and pay for it yourself." Although it can be grueling to watch, and even more painful to resist interfering, try to remember *if we allow our children to fail, we are allowing them to grow.*

Resisting the temptation to enable our children is tough but doable. The harsher alternative is having a son or daughter who lacks the skills to take care of themselves, well after we've gone to heaven. Rather than sit at home and be tempted to control, give your children some breathing room. Allow them to focus on their careers, to cultivate friendships, and to enrich their own relationships.

If they have children, allow them to be the parents. Enjoy being the grandparent who provides unconditional love, offering little advice, *unless asked.* The temptation to control and say, "Here's what I would do" is oh so hard, but remember, the enemy wants to cause division in your family. *Trust me, I speak from experience.* My mouth has gotten me into a whole heap of trouble on more than one occasion. While I'd love to tell my grown daughters, "Oh just wait, you'll see," I've learned to fall upon my sword and ask for forgiveness.

As Christian parents, we must allow God to handle the big teaching moments. It is simply not our job. Don't feel guilty for choosing other activities to fill up your time. It doesn't mean you love your children less; it means you simply trust them more. You trust them to make their own decisions and are willing to live with the consequences. You trust that your years of Christian parenting will be evident as they raise their own children.

Their actions may not be what you'd choose for yourself, but you are not them. Allow them to marvel in their uniqueness, and above all, to be secure in the person God has created them to be. It's all about trusting God. Escape from the worry by allowing God to be in charge of your family's life.

He knows the story, so allow Him to write the chapters.

I've saved the most serious means of escape for the end of this chapter. It is my prayer that if this pertains to you, perhaps you might go on a long walk and ask yourself, "Could this be me?" Please know that's all I'm asking of you at this point—*simply think about it.* But taking this first step is critical in stopping a temptation from turning into an addiction. I hope you feel me holding your sweet hand.

The statistics cause all of us to shake our heads in confusion. The National Center for Health Statistics found that over 69,000 people died of drug overdose in 2019, with the number jumping to over 106,000 in 2021.[6] Of course, we are all aware of the dangers of heroin, cocaine, methamphetamine, and other illicit drugs, which definitely deserve serious attention. However, that's not what troubles me the most.

While millions of us take a fierce stance against drugs like heroin, many cannot admit to abusing prescription drugs or alcohol.

6. Merianne Rose Spencer, et al., "Drug Overdose Deaths in the United States, 2001–2021," National Center for Health Statistics, *NCHS Data Brief No. 457,* December 2022, www.cdc.gov/nchs/products/databriefs/db457.htm.

Why the denial? Because then we'd have to own our deep insecurities and pain.

JESSICA'S STORY

Jessica woke up from her back surgery and felt better than she'd felt in years. Although her surgeon had prescribed a narcotic for postoperative pain, she only used a couple pills, as they made her feel too sleepy and out of control. A few weeks later, Jessica's oldest son announced he was dropping out of college and would like to move back home. Shocked and upset, Jessica and her husband felt they had no choice but to allow it. They also began arguing more, insisting their son get a job to contribute to their finances. Unable to sleep one evening, Jessica decided to take one of the pain pills she'd kept after her surgery. It wasn't long until every time Jessica and her husband argued about finances, she'd retreat to her bedroom and take one of her pain pills. She began to hide them in her purse, fearing she'd be somewhere without them. The temptation to escape and forget her problems had become too hard to resist.

Let me be the first to say that I understand the need for prescription medications. I experience debilitating pain that causes me to rely on specific medications for relief. However, they can be relied upon too much—and the enemy is always waiting to pounce upon our weaknesses—so I prefer to use pain patches.

As with many addictive behaviors, our brain doesn't know when to say *no*, especially if a drug is relieving our pain while also releasing feel-good dopamine. Besides brain chemistry, women need to realize that drug and alcohol addictions can have a stronger effect on them than men. Sisters, please pay attention.

- ✦ It takes a smaller amount of a drug, as well as less time using it, for women to become addicted.
- ✦ Women are more likely to relapse after treatment.
- ✦ Sex hormones can make women more sensitive than men to the effects of some drugs.
- ✦ Women who use drugs will experience more physical effects on their heart and blood vessels.
- ✦ Women who are victims of domestic violence are at increased risk of substance use.
- ✦ Divorce, loss of child custody, or the death of a partner or child can trigger women's substance abuse, which is also connected to serious mental health disorders.
- ✦ Women who abuse pain medications may be more likely to have panic attacks, anxiety, or depression.

These are troubling statistics. Rather than step into the light and wrestle with such consequences, many prefer to stay in the dark and self-medicate. It's the ultimate escape candy with far-reaching repercussions. I've spoken with hundreds of women who struggled with addiction. All of them shared a common response after falling into temptation with prescription drugs: the abuse landed them in extreme isolation and further pain. They fell victim to a deadly trifecta—they longed to feel needed, they yearned to escape, and, worst of all, they were experiencing real physical pain. Life's sucker punches tempt women to stay down on the mat and whisper, "I give up. You win."

What then?

For many, the answer is to abuse alcohol rather than prescription medications. Even worse is the choice to abuse both. The combination can be deadly. Some use the excuse that a glass of merlot can take the edge off a brutal day at the office. Or perhaps we tell ourselves that no one could possibly understand what we endure at home, so a few cocktails are warranted. And friend, if you did not partake in one or four glasses of wine during the COVID-19 nightmare, you're a stronger woman than me. Statistics show that the use of alcohol during that catastrophe quadrupled. Reread that. *Quadrupled.* Sadly, it makes perfect sense. We needed a way to process fear and frustration that was far beyond our control.

But excuses can only carry us so far. Accountability has to take place at some point.

REBECCA'S STORY

Rebecca, age forty-eight, was absolutely drained. During the COVID nightmare, she'd had to learn how to homeschool her fourteen-year-old daughter Jackie, who was trying her every nerve. After previously punishing Jackie for being on the computer too much, Rebecca now found herself telling her to get on the computer and finish her homework. After taking Jackie's phone away due to rude behavior, Rebecca gave up and retreated to her bedroom with a glass of wine. She'd been laid off from her job due to cutbacks and had no idea what to do with her daughter. It didn't help matters that Jackie's father was not in the picture at all. A few glasses of wine each night eventually turned into an entire bottle—anything to help take the edge off Rebecca's nerves.

She had to have something to help her forget her mounting problems.

Like so many temptations that turn into habits, then addictions, it doesn't take long for that one drink or pill to feel insufficient. Our brains begin to crave more and more. One extra pain pill becomes three, and that evening glass of wine turns into two glasses of scotch. Of course, no one willingly chooses to become addicted. We know better. There's too much information out there for us to claim ignorance.

Unlike using illicit drugs and breaking the law, we only have to show proof of our age to purchase alcohol and can obtain legal prescriptions from doctors. We tell ourselves that we truly *need* these things or *deserve* them. Some may become incensed when someone in their circle cares enough to bring up the possibility of an addiction. *How dare they?* But we all know denial is very common. It's easy for the accused to reply, "What are you talking about? You're crazy! I'm not hooked on anything!" We can deny addiction until we're blue in the face but that doesn't stop millions of women from going to the pharmacy, stopping at the liquor store, and getting high. Before you go another second being physically or emotionally harmed due to substance abuse, you can move past the denial and take that first step. *You can do this, sweet friend. You can.*

While I enjoy wine with a nice Italian meal, I've learned to stop after one glass. That's it. No more. While it's fairly easy for me to slow down, I know it's difficult for others. Each person's thought process is complicated. Genetics, our resolve to quit, our strength in the struggle against the enemy—all of these factors play a critical role. We are all just one step away from making a poor choice that can lead us down a rabbit hole.

But regardless of the circumstances, you can wrestle it to the ground once and for all. Even if you're sipping on your third glass of chardonnay as you read this very book, Jesus adores you and wants to help you stop this. Let that sink deep into your heart.

Jesus longs to help you get well and be the flat-out incredible woman He designed you to be!

Weaning oneself off of alcohol or prescription drugs results in the following health benefits:

1. Improved skin tone, less wrinkles, and more collagen

2. Better sleep

3. The ability to lose weight easier

4. Improved mental health

5. Lower risk of cancer

6. Lower risk of cardiovascular issues

7. Better memory and thinking

It is my prayer that reading these dramatic results is a big enough wake-up call for you to say, "Okay, girl, that's enough." I fully realize that's not the case for everyone. I know many women, some close friends, who tell themselves, "This is my life, and I'll just take the risk. I'm fine with that." But we know that's not true. It's simply too difficult to stop.

As a raw and real writer who's consulted with many counselors and qualified physicians, I'm going to tell you that it might require more than prayer to break your addiction. God offers up qualified professionals to us for a reason. Brain chemistry is a very real part of our body's makeup, and sometimes medication is needed to balance things a bit. *That's a conversation between you and your clinician.*

We must gather our superwoman strength and admit we have given in to harmful cravings. You are not alone in this. Remember, as you read this book, you're among friends who totally get you. Even though we are guilty as charged, we have a pardoner in Jesus. God knew we'd mess up all along, which is exactly why His Son repeatedly whispers, *"I forgive you. I'm not going anywhere. You can do this, and I'm still crazy about you."*

Isn't that absolutely amazing?! He will celebrate every little victory with us, whether it's going without alcohol or drugs for six days or six years. You deserve a healthy mind that thinks clearly and a body that can wiggle in celebration of all you've accomplished.

You got this. More importantly, *He has you.*

5

THE STICKY WEB

I am not a fan of spiders. Never have been, never will be. But I *am* intrigued.

While they're not usually in the running for the *most beautiful animal* or *cutest creature* in the world, some of them are incredibly colorful.

The eight spotted crab spider is a cheerful lemon color that almost looks more like a piece of candy than an arachnid. Like its name, this vivid yellow spider is spotted, although not always with eight spots. As it ages, it gets even more spots…sorta like us menopausal women who struggle with them on our hands or face. Have mercy. That provides me zero consolation.

A real stunner is the peacock spider. It flaunts an incredible rainbow of colors that shines iridescently in the light. Its abdomen looks like a peacock feather, colored with blue, aquamarine, turquoise, green, and orange stripes. There are at least ninety-two species of peacock spiders recorded, and all but one live in Australia. Sorry, Aussieland, but that may be reason enough for me to just buy a postcard. To impress a female spider, the male peacock spider flattens out a section of his colorful abdomen like a large fan, raising his hind legs above him and waving them side to side. This dance could last up to an hour before the female decides whether he is a worthy mate—and if she remains unimpressed, she has the option to eat him.

Ha! God love those picky female spiders! They chew up and spit out males who don't agree with them.

But the spider with which I'm most intrigued is the ladybird mimic spider. It has almost the exact color pattern of a ladybug beetle, known as ladybird beetles in the United Kingdom. It's easy to mistake this spider for an actual ladybug. While many animals avoid eating ladybugs since these beneficial beetles can make them sick, they do eat spiders. So to avoid predators, the ladybird mimic spider makes itself look like a ladybug, curling its small head and petite legs under its large abdomen to ward off would-be predators. Talk about sneaky!

Of course, spider webs are just as fascinating. Spider silk isn't just strong; it's super resilient. As elastic as rubber, some spider silk can stretch up to four times its original length without breaking. Their composition is often compared to synthetic fibers like Kevlar—you know, the stuff used to make bulletproof vests.

It's no wonder the creators of the Internet chose to use the term World Wide Web.

Oh, how this web has done a number on our minds, our hearts, and our very lives. Just like the ladybird mimic spider, *websites* can morph into whatever is required to achieve their objective. They spin a web so sneaky that with one click, we are drawn in…until we are trapped with no means of escape, often left emotionally or financially wrecked.

The most harmful predator on the Internet is, of course, social media. It's colorful, tracks our every step, and tears our self-worth into pieces. The carnage it creates is so far-reaching that I can't help but devote two chapters to its seriousness. Hang on.

Sadly, we have subconsciously learned to base our value on the opinions of individuals who view our photos or videos for an average of ten seconds. *Ten seconds!*

Before we assume this solely pertains to millennials and their TikTok videos, you might want to sit down for this next bit of data. According to the Nielsen Total Audience Report for April 2020, adults ages fifty to sixty-four are the most avid media consumers, spending 13 hours and 50 minutes connected to media, which is over twice as much time as adults ages thirty-five to forty-nine.[7] Back up, ladies. Go back and reread that.

If women our age are consuming media more than others, we're allowing it to affect our emotional health to a greater extent as well.

Facts don't lie. And yet we wonder why serious communication—*talking and even intimacy*—is lacking in our relationships, leading to more dysfunction than ever.

Whether we like to admit it or not, the need for attention has wormed its way into every part of our lives. This desperate

---

7. *The Nielsen Total Audience Report: April 2020,* www.nielsen.com/insights/2020/the-nielsen-total-audience-report-april-2020.

need to be noticed plays a critical role in the indulgence of temptations of every kind.

Barbara Denevers, a noted psychiatric nurse practitioner in Los Alamos, told me:

> Our craving to feel acknowledged is often due to the lack of having real loving relationships which involve real time with other human beings. Real face time is desperately needed, not just screen time on a phone or laptop. Sadly, one will perform activities to the extreme, risking embarrassment and regret, anything to receive the attention they crave.

One of the most troubling trends is that of young women posting pornographic images of themselves, hanging their worth on the comments of total strangers, all while putting their very lives at risk. It's heartbreaking that women would reveal themselves to strangers and expose themselves to potential stalkers rather than refrain from posting a thirty-second video on TikTok.

I cannot imagine raising teenage daughters in this insecurity-inducing hailstorm. This incessant craving for attention now starts while a child is in diapers. I've seen three-year-olds work an iPad better than I can. By the time they're teenagers, their psyche has endured so many dents of insecurity that counselors are on speed dial. It is absolutely heartbreaking to watch the lengths to which young girls go for a thumbs-up, heart emoji, or, sadly, a flirtatious message from *a fan*.

We shouldn't be surprised at this downward spiral. After all, the first stars on social media became famous for their videos showing them having sex. My friends, we need to pray incessantly that today's young women will realize they're being duped. I'm convinced it's no surprise that the logo on my phone is a piece of fruit with a bite taken out of it. Adam and Eve were lured away by the same.

Sadly, many mothers use a common excuse to justify their daughter's actions: "I want my daughter to feel empowered and comfortable to express herself." Go tell that to a parent whose child was catfished, stalked, and raped as a result of being online. Tell that to a mother who just admitted her daughter to an anorexia treatment center because she measured herself against Photoshopped females. This craving for perfection and attention does *not* have to be the new normal.

If you are a mother or grandmother who tends to look the other way, thinking, "That's just how kids are these days," I beg you to wake up from the shell shock. Out of love, I must say that perhaps your own war with insecurity is still being waged. Don't hand off those battles to the next generation. I've been on that battlefield—and it is bloody and brutal.

Parents, regardless of their ages, take note of what your children are doing on social media.

It's easy to close the door and ignore their posts...until it's too late. The enemy lives on social media, waiting for flirtatious hashtags that hint of vulnerability. Sadly, the pandemic of the early 2020s added gasoline to an already smoldering fire. Compound kids' reliance on social media with the years lacking in real socialization, and the result is an inferno worse than any prior disaster. I pray every day for the kids who missed recesses full of giggles, high school game nights, and maskless college move-ins. Socialization skills have suffered greatly, and it will be years before we see the full fallout.

Whether young or old, social media plays a dominant role in the development of our self-esteem, whether we choose to admit it or not. Perhaps it's because I'm a former high school teacher and mother to two adult daughters, but this is an issue that tears my heart out. Young women are struggling with insecurity so fiercely that their acrylic nails are ready to pop off.

It reminds me of an event I once witnessed as a high school teacher.

Cafeteria duty is one of the least favorite assignments that teachers receive from a principal. While others may think teachers are getting a free period, it's actually more like a whack-a-mole game. It's a constant struggle trying to stop trouble from popping up where you least suspect it—especially when hormonal teenagers are involved.

One Thursday (yes, I still remember the day of this sad affair), I noticed one of my female students giving an icy stare to another girl across the cafeteria. It was so cold even *I* felt it. The young blond girl casting the stare may have weighed one hundred pounds, soaking wet. She came from a wealthy family, was dating a hunk on the basketball team, and had an enormous chip on her shoulder. I could see the outrage in those blue eyes of hers from across the way.

The recipient of her icy stare was another student who was as tall as most guys, a bit of a loudmouth who hung out with an intimidating group of seniors. After a few minutes of exchanging stares colder than Dirty Harry's, the one-hundred-pound blond walked over and broke a lunch tray over the other girl's head. Mind you, this tray held a bowl of vegetable soup and the best peach cobbler on the planet. Peaches hit the wall as quickly as the potatoes and carrots. It took only seconds for the girls to get into one of the worst fights I'd ever seen. The recipient of the tray, who ended up with a slight concussion, was not anticipating the sneak attack. A tussle ensued as hair flew, nails popped off, and faces got bloodied because both girls were wearing rings.

And what did I do as the teacher on duty?

I just stood there.

I was terrified, knowing full well I didn't have the strength to separate them. Thankfully, the football coach came to my rescue. While preparing to haul the two prize fighters to the principal's office, I couldn't help but raise my voice and ask, "What in the *world* is wrong with you two?! What brought this on?!" Their reply still causes me to shake my head today. The little sprite of a girl vented, "She was looking at my boyfriend and I will *not* have it. She's trying to steal him from me and I'm going to kick her..."

Well, you get the picture. The recipient of the broken tray, still dizzy from the crash, shouted back, "You crazy %^&$! Anyway, if I could get his attention, then you never had him in the first place!"

I tell you, friend, I didn't know whether to laugh or cry. I glanced over at the male student responsible for the fur a flyin' and, of course, he did what any guy would do who'd just watched two girls lose hair and nails over him. My dad used to call it "walking around like the cock of the rock." He walked around the school that day as if he were George Clooney or Chris Hemsworth. Sheesh.

My heart broke for those two girls. I had the most sympathy for the tiny Muhammad Ali of tray breaking. Since she was one of my students, I'd seen her constantly looking in the mirror at herself during class. She was a nervous wreck when taking a test. I'd met her mom and dad at parent-teacher conferences and clearly got the clue they expected perfection. In addition to wielding a food-filled tray, this young girl had been hit over the head for years with a big ol' insecurity hammer. She was likely peppered with harsh words and ridicule from parents, friends, or both. It's been over twenty years since that incident, and I pray she's talked to God about it. If not, I have a feeling others may be the recipient of her insecurity and shame today. Rather than breaking trays, she's probably broken hearts more than once, including her own.

I cannot imagine the fallout of such a high school throw-down, had the students owned smart phones and used social media as they do today. Instead of sixty students watching two girls make fools of themselves, it would have been more like six thousand. The spectacle would be on the Internet for all eternity, for their future children to see.

Hiring managers at some of the country's biggest companies admit that they considered social media posts prior to offering a job to someone. Whether we like it or not, the social media semitrucks have barreled their way into every household in America. The owners of these death traps aren't losing a wink of sleep over the destroyed lives they leave lying beside the road.

I've watched roundtables with psychologists and parents on how to fix this nightmare, for today's young women have an off-the-charts chance of falling victim to temptation, shame, and addiction. The odds of them experiencing depression and anxiety are all but guaranteed.

In addition to the dismantling of one's self-worth, the enemy is also using social media to create a division so wide that it keeps me up at night. I pray fervently for God to heal this great nation. I'm also praying for Him to grab this author by her little blond head and protect her from this temptation. Mercy! Know, girlfriends, I am throwing myself under the bus with you.

At one time or another, many women have been lured in and fallen to the temptation of posting opinions online to anyone who will read them. Oh, friend, the enemy has twisted our minds into such knots that I pray we can unwind and walk in a straight path.

Women (and men) must keep one critical thing in mind: *it's called social media for a reason.* If you post your view on a topic, be prepared for someone to disagree with you. Fair is fair if you are choosing to give your two cents. Try to remind yourself repeatedly, "Just because I have an opinion doesn't mean I have to give it. I will not burst into flames if I turn the other cheek and refuse to comment."

Oh, friend, we must remember that every single thing we read online is not directed at us personally. It reminds me of a story I heard recently that emphasizes this very point. A guy went to a small public park and posted a sign that he was going to start giving guitar lessons. Within five minutes, a visitor stormed into the park, saw the sign, and screamed out loud, "Doesn't he know I don't even play the guitar!?"

I couldn't help but giggle at this truth. We read every post on social media and apply it directly to ourselves. Excuse my bluntness, friends, but we are *not* the center of the universe. It's not all about us. It's all about Jesus.

The sooner we accept the fact that Jesus's opinion is all that matters, the kinder our hearts—and the calmer our nerves—will become.

There *is* hope. In conducting research for this book, I interviewed many young adults who proudly now consider themselves *clean and sober* from social media. After having hearts broken, reputations shattered, or being passed over for jobs due to inappropriate posts still lingering in the stratosphere, many are ignoring social media altogether.

LEAVING FAKE FILTERED FRIENDS BEHIND

One twenty-seven-year-old woman put it this way:

I wanted to be seen, liked, and loved on social media. I wanted to be noticed. If that didn't happen, I went with my next best option—the shock or the stupid. That's what my friends and I call it. Eventually, I got bored with social media because I only met fake filtered friends. I'm so over trying to look like a pinup girl. Anyway, I'm starting to value my privacy. I don't want everyone knowing my business.

Hallelujah! I pray this young lady's attitude goes viral. Let's learn this valuable lesson from the youth of the day. These God-fearing men and women are our future. Pray for them. Pray that they grow in number. I praise my holy Father for giving me two daughters who've turn their noses up at social media for the most part. They have better things to do, preferring to focus on their faith, marriages, and careers.

I'll cut to the chase: we've binged on the artificial candy called *social media* long enough and have suffered some serious psychological side effects. Just like eating junk food that lands on our thighs, we have to face reality and get clear eyed, *sans* a photo filter.

Together, let's resist the temptation to comment on every post with which we disagree. Together, let's be diligent in protecting our loved ones from spider webs that devour their self-worth. Arm in arm, let's stand up to the enemy's traps that are disguised as harmless posts.

We know better. The only person you need approval from is a Man named Jesus. He's your biggest fan. Our Savior not only *likes* you, He *loves* you with more heart emojis than you can count on both hands.

6

FORBIDDEN FRUIT

This chapter is not an easy conversation to have.

While we've discussed some very real insecurities and cravings that affect us emotionally, some temptations begin in our minds but play out in other parts of our bodies. It's also the reason this chapter is longer than others: it affects millions of women. Of all the temptations mentioned in the Bible, sexual temptation is mentioned more than any other. Of course, add social media and binge-worthy TV to this temptation, and a woman's mind conjures up the steamiest of fantasies.

Perhaps you've read a similar passage or watched it on screen:

He rode in on horseback, releasing a guttural sound in earshot of her captors. It was evident that no one would steal her away from him without a fight. After crushing anyone who would dare do her harm, he whisked her away to a safe

*place and made passionate love to her by the fire, satisfying
her wildest desires. She was safe now...and totally fulfilled.*

Of course, this erotic passage is pure fiction, yet women fall
for it time and again. Who wouldn't want to be swept away, val-
iantly fought for, passionately made love to, and taken on some
great around-the-world adventure? We want the total package,
all tied up with a sexy red satin bow. Many of us crave it so
desperately that we'll do anything to meet that deep yearning
simmering beneath our skin. Unfortunately, if these physical
desires aren't met, some women do whatever it takes to feel
temporarily satisfied. This includes indulging in *candy* ranging
from binge-watching pornography to engaging in inappropriate
relationships.

While the previous chapter focused on social media and
its effect on the psyche of all women, this chapter takes an up
close and personal look at its impact on marriage and intimate
relationships. Dangerous temptations surrounding social media
deserve two chapters. It's that big of a deal.

Regardless of whether we try to justify our reading explicit
books or content, watching explicit sex scenes on a binge-worthy
series, or secretly viewing pornography on our smart phones, the
consequences can be extremely troublesome to our hearts, minds,
and bodies. Meaningful fulfillment is rarely experienced with such
artificially sweet temptations. Still, many indulge in it regularly,
thinking it might satisfy some longing, even if temporary. I'm
afraid, my friend, contentment and cravings are two sides of the
same piercing sword.

SUSAN'S STORY

Married for twenty-seven years, Susan was excited that both she and her husband were now retired. Their son was happily married, had his own family, and lived six hours away. Susan and Tom now had lots of time on their hands. While reading used to be her favorite hobby, she recently found a bunch of steamy TV shows that piqued her interest. Tom watched football games in his man cave and usually turned in early. Over the years, they'd both gained a significant amount of weight and neither was very interested in intimacy. On a more regular basis, Susan found herself searching for TV shows that were sexually charged, with sex scenes being dominant. She also began to get angry that she and her husband hardly ever had sex. After six months of watching one steamy show after another, Susan wanted more. After her husband went to bed, she began putting her phone on private mode and watching pornography. With each click, Susan wondered why she and her husband never had sex like she saw on screen. She also became angry with herself for caving in to watch it. As a Christian, Susan assumed God had stopped listening to her prayers and was totally disgusted with her actions. She quit going to church and even stopped praying. Overwhelmed with shame, Susan wished she could go to sleep and never wake up.

I wish I could say this was a rare conversation I heard while conducting research for this book. But this was a story I heard often from brave women desperate to get healthy. Before we wade further into this sensitive topic, I realize there are many women who may read the title of this chapter and think, "Nah, this part doesn't pertain to me." If that is you, girlfriend, I salute you and thank God for your strength. However, with the *spicy* rating of recommended books on TikTok and the explicit nature of shows readily available on all our streaming services, we have to realize that pornography is no longer reserved for magazines or certain websites.

You've grasped the words of theologians like Charles Spurgeon, who warned, "Like the old knights in wartime, we must sleep with helmet and breastplate buckled on, for the arch-deceiver will seize our first unguarded hour to make us his prey."[8]

Sadly, many have found themselves in a situation like Susan's. At one time or another, women forgot about the protection God said they'd need to navigate this evil world. The consequences of such forgetfulness are far from pretty. The weight of temptation and guilt can sink a woman's self-worth quicker than the *Titanic*. If you desire a romantic relationship that won't be riddled with "Why did I watch *that*?" or "If only he'd do *this* to me," then keep reading. *We gotta get real, girlfriends, and come clean.*

While steering from these temptations may be as painful as whipping off a bandage, if done with compassion, it can allow for a healing that might not even leave a scar. But before we can take that first step in the right direction, we must address the big question looming inside hearts, not to mention the other parts of our bodies: *Why is there a greater need for sexual satisfaction as we women get older?*

---

8. Charles Spurgeon, *Morning and Evening* (New Kensington, PA: Whitaker House, 2002), 115.

Sexual frustration is just that—frustrating—and it's nothing to be ashamed of. According to psychologists who have middle-aged women as the bulk of their patients, women ages forty-five to sixty are the group who most often complain of not having enough sex with their spouse. Can I get an *amen* on that?! Let's try and make some sense of this.

As women go through menopause, changes of every kind often take place. Grown children usually leave the home, we become more comfortable with our bodies, and the risk of pregnancy decreases. It's a trifecta pointing to sexual cravings and the need to be satisfied. We may even become more willing to engage in activities with our spouse that we dared not consider previously. At this uninhibited stage of life, we begin to finally figure out who we are and what we want. Hallelujah, right?! But it's also at this time we often wonder if God is trying to play some kind of cruel joke.

Around the same time a woman develops stronger cravings for more frequent and meaningful sex, a man's desire for intimacy often *decreases* at the same age. Yes, you read that correctly. Pressures ranging from career demands, financial responsibilities, and even erectile dysfunction often play a role in decreasing men's desire for sex.

As a result of such opposing needs, many couples become frustrated and choose to isolate themselves, anything to avoid discussing this very sensitive and yet critical issue. I've heard several friends comment, "My husband and I are just roommates. We've been together for over twenty-five years and I'm *so* over having steamy sex. That fizzled out years ago. I'd rather curl up with a good book." Sadly, the fallout of such seclusion can often lead to overdosing on *artificial sweets*, giving in to the urges that harm one's body and soul, such as pornography, extramarital affairs, and inappropriate online relationships.

What causes us to fall victim to such behavior? *Let me be clear, it's not just middle-aged women who struggle with sexual temptation.* I've spoken to women ages twenty-five to seventy who struggle with this issue. Perhaps a woman has only been married for a few years, the new has worn off, and she's searching for that continual sizzle. Rather than hurt the person she loves, she chooses to binge-watch a racy TV show or visit a porn site and quench her cravings by watching someone else. After all, it's not as bad as having an affair…or at least that's the lie she tells herself. With access to hundreds of channels on TV, there's a show to tempt pretty much anyone. From sexually charged shows starring Vikings or vixens to Italian heartthrobs with air-brushed muscles, millions of women sink into the sofa and enjoy their *screen candy* every week.

And just like the addiction to shopping, alcohol, or anything else, the brain keeps wanting more and more dopamine. *Feeling good is not enough; it wants to feel great all the time.* As a result, women take their favorite show into their own bedroom or someone else's, trying to mentally feed their urges with great desperation. It's only after leaving a secret meeting place or facing the truth of their lie that some women get angry.

Rather than feel shame and regret, it's easier to become angry at one's spouse for not possessing the steamy attributes for which they've fantasized. I'm sure you can sense the downward spiral that follows. Perhaps you're haunted by the pain of your own downward journey. Perhaps you're still angry, feeling no one understands, and prefer to stick to your old habits.

Perhaps "I'm not hurting anyone" is the lie you whisper to yourself as tears of regret roll down your face.

God is here with you, I promise.

With the ability to binge-watch a steamy TV show or pornography for hours on end, it's easy to get pulled into a fake reality. The brain releases dopamine for longer periods of time, and it's easier to become addicted. If you feel such behavior could never apply to you, take notice. It can creep in and be almost as harmful as alcohol or prescription pills.

To those who feel I've exposed your dark secret, please don't think you're being ostracized. If anything, read these statistics from Enough Is Enough,[9] an organization dedicated to making the Internet safer for children and families. It will reinforce the knowledge that you're not alone:

- 47 percent of Christians say that pornography is a problem in the home.

- 34 percent of Christian women struggle with an addiction to pornography.

- 60 percent of the women who answered the survey admitted to having significant struggles with lust. Forty percent of this group admitted to being involved in sexual sin in the past year.

- More than 80 percent of women with pornography addiction take it offline by acting out their behaviors in real life, such as having multiple partners, casual sex, or affairs.

- 56 percent of divorces involve one party having an *obsessive interest* in pornographic websites.

---

9. Enough Is Enough, enough.org.

Ladies, if you're part of these statistics, please know that the temptation to watch pornography can grow into an addiction faster than you realize. This is due, in large part, to the vast array of free online porn. Once you begin watching, the addiction takes hold due to the dopamine high we've already discussed. If the addiction progresses, the free Internet pornography you sneak and watch soon won't be enough. The enemy is clever. He will not only make you want more, he'll cause you to empty your bank account.

Given that pornography addictions often morph into marital infidelity, neither party in a marriage escapes the fallout. The addict feels guilt and embarrassment over their inability to stop, and the spouse feels rage, betrayal, and humiliation. Physical intimacy all but disappears, and divorce is often the final consequence.

With this evidence, I pray you'll think twice before picking up that TV remote or opening your web browser. But remember this, dear one: You are not alone. You're among millions of others in the midst of a struggle. The second half of this book is going to help you wrestle these sexual temptations to the ground and never look back.

Many men and women often take their need for attention and intimacy past that of steamy TV shows and pornography. Perhaps you're in a relationship where real sexual intimacy has always been a problem. Without thinking it through, you try to satisfy your needs by engaging in an extramarital affair.

Sneaking around, telling lies, and having sex with someone other than your spouse does nothing but cause heartache and hostility for everyone involved. Sure, the dopamine high takes place, and you have trouble ending the affair, often for that very reason alone. But just like all other addictions, you're left feeling shame, guilt, and emptiness. Of course, the effects these indiscretions have on children could be a book in itself.

TRACI'S STORY

At age fifty-nine, Traci had been divorced for three years. As a Christian, she had wanted to work things out, but her husband was not willing and moved on with his life. Tracey felt like she'd failed her church, her parents, and even her children. Fast approaching sixty, she believed no man would ever be attracted to her again. One evening, while scrolling on a social media site, a male work colleague messaged her. After a few weeks of conversing with him online, Eric mentioned he'd always been attracted to her and thought she was beautiful. He wished they could meet in private. But upon finding out he was married, Traci immediately cut off all communication with Eric. After a few weeks, however, she missed his flirtatious compliments and messaged Eric again. Soon, their messaging escalated into sexual conversations, and Traci agreed to meet him at a hotel. Six months later, at Traci's workplace, Eric's wife stormed in and confronted her with printed copies of conversations and photos she'd found on his computer. Word of Eric and Traci's affair spread all over town. Traci found herself too embarrassed to go to church and felt like a failure to her kids, not to mention her parents. She had never felt so alone and wished she could run away.

Like many women, Traci learned the hard way that relationships of substance have *nothing* to do with screens, and everything to do with actual laughing, holding hands, emotional conversations, and enjoying loving sex with a partner. The temptation to interact with others on social media affects every part of our lives. Every. Single. One. But as I've said previously, resisting the temptation is tough. Oh, the enemy knows our triggers and just when to pull them. If a woman feels trapped in a relationship that lacks intimacy and laughter, she'll be tempted to turn to her phone or computer for a temporary fix for attention. Women, just like men, will overindulge in *fake sweets* that do nothing but poison their hearts and minds.

As evidenced in the all-too-common story of Traci, no one is immune from falling victim to sexual indiscretion online or offline, including Christians. We are as human and fallible as anyone else. In fact, according to the *Journal of Psychology and Christianity*, an average of 65 percent of men and 55 percent of women will have an extramarital affair by the time they are forty years old.[10]

In his book *Torn Asunder: Recovering from Extramarital Affairs*,[11] pastor and therapist Dave Carder identifies four types of affairs:

+ Class I – the one-night stand

---

10. Cindy Crosby, "Why Affairs Happen. And what you need to know about prevention and recovery," *Today's Christian Woman*, September 2008, www.todayschristianwoman.com/articles/2008/september/why-affairs-happen.html.
11. Dave Carder with Duncan Jaenicke, *Torn Asunder: Recovering from Extramarital Affairs* (Chicago, IL: Moody Press, 2008).

+ Class II – the entangled affair, lasting eighteen to twenty-four months; it may start as a friendship that grows due to a deficit in the marriage

+ Class III – sexual addiction, involving multiple partners, lasting years, with periods of binge behavior; a history of molestation or sexual activity before puberty may be a factor

+ Class IV – the add-on affair, long-term but irregular, with sporadic contact

Carder says Class II and Class IV affairs "always involve emotional and sexual entanglement. In these types, the man and woman have a relationship often akin to the marriage relationship…The entangled affair is neither a one-night fling (Class I) nor an extended pattern of addictive behavior (Class III), both of which usually show only minimal relationship development."

When one or both in a marriage have a deep history of pain that's related to sex in some way, an extramarital affair is often an unsuccessful means of covering up long-held anguish.

But the temptation to have an affair, in and of itself, is much less obvious. There are no signs flashing or alarms screaming, "Warning! Don't do this! Run in the other direction!" *If only it were that easy to detect.* When talking with women who have engaged in extramarital relationships, they often say their initial interactions with the other person seemed innocent and justifiable.

But that's exactly how the enemy works.

Perhaps, like so many, you have already ignored the signposts and taken your heart over a cliff. It was only *after* the deed had been done that you realized you carelessly gave the most intimate part of yourself to someone who didn't care as much as you'd hoped.

Dear one, that doesn't mean you are beyond redemption. You may feel you've ventured down so many wrong alleys, there's zero chance in finding your way back. You've berated yourself into believing you're the last woman on earth who deserves happiness or forgiveness. But know this: nothing could be further from the truth. Own that, my friend. Reread it if you must.

Be filled with optimism about the wonderful future God has in store for you!

There is no such thing as different levels of sin warranting different degrees of punishment.

Even if we think that's how the world should operate, we aren't the ones in charge. Thank You, merciful Jesus!

Whether it's engaging in an affair, being addicted to porn, or abusing drugs or alcohol, Jesus loves you and wants to make you whole. No more hiding in a dark corner and crying in shame. You can and you will resist the temptation with the help of Jesus Christ. *Refuse to go back to the dark by remembering the awful pain you suffered.* Ask God for strength and thank Him for grace. No more going backward for you!

The second half of this book is going to put you on the path to sweet freedom, and that includes acquiring 20/20 vision. You'll clearly see the difference between the human need for sexual intimacy versus the snares of sexual temptation. We are going to talk about it *all*, and that includes how to explain your sexual needs to your partner. *As I've said already, it's time to get real.*

Now, go splash some cold water on your face, fix your hair, and put on a little lipstick. Grab my hand, sweet girl. We're doing to step into the light together and grasp the beauty of being a woman of God.

It's about darn time.

PART TWO

A HEALTHY APPETITE

As soon as you eat the fruit and hit guilt,
shame, frustration, the Enemy changes roles.
He shifts from being the enticer and promiser to
becoming the accuser and the condemner.
—Louie Giglio, *Don't Give the Enemy a Seat at Your
Table*

7

THE SHAME GAME

Perhaps this chapter should be in stereo surround sound to emphasize its importance. Be prepared, my friend. This chapter has many musical references.

Anyone who knows me well is aware of how much I love music of all genres. My favorites range from Lauren Daigle, Chris Tomlin, and Casting Crowns to Third Eye Blind, Little Big Town, and Counting Crows. Don't judge. I like variety.

Since obtaining my driver's license in the Stone Age, I've often felt the most free when cruising down the road alone. What sixteen-year-old doesn't remember driving with the windows open, hair blowing in the wind, and singing at the top of their lungs to one of their favorite songs. Years later, when driving my daughters to school, I'd often ask them to keep their voices down whenever one of my top ten favorites played on the radio. Without fail, I'd get the dreaded eye roll, reminding me that my *top ten favorites* was actually a list of fifty or sixty. You can imagine my elation when I get into their cars now and hear those same songs on their playlist. Ah, we mothers have to grab what victories we can.

Five years ago, singing was the absolute last thing on my mind. Rather than belting out happy tunes, I was white-knuckling my Bible, searching for answers. After years of struggle and counseling sessions, my marriage had grown colder than the north winds of Taos, New Mexico. We mutually agreed it was not salvageable and filed for divorce. I was in more pieces than the piñata I mentioned in chapter one. Living in a small town, the rumors were rampant—some of them truthful, some so facetious that I questioned the sanity of those who concocted such yarns.

Alone in an adobe, 1,300 miles from my grown children, the only constant was that by the end of the day, I'd be throwing up in my bathroom toilet. I was sick with fear, unsure of where I'd live or what I'd do with my life. On a regular basis, the room swirled, the tears fell, and part of me wanted to die. But through strength from God, not to mention support from a few friends who love me unabashedly, I gained composure.

Often, I'd go for a drive and play music by Casting Crowns. That's when I heard it. If you haven't, for the love of women everywhere, you should. Go and give it a listen now.

Does anybody hear her?

Can anybody see?

Or does anybody even know she's going down today?[12]

Friends, I had no choice but to pull off to the side of the road and cry big ugly tears. I felt her. *I was her.* I was going down, and

---

12. Casting Crowns, "Does Anybody Hear Her," on *Lifesong* (Beach Street, Reunion, PLG, 2006).

I was drowning in shame that I could not make my marriage work. I needed hope, somehow, somewhere. Sadly, the compassion of some was overshadowed by the judgment of others. There is something seriously wrong if women feel shame in the very place where they should be uplifted and loved. I pray you've never been a recipient of lofty glances, although I'm betting you have. I have a feeling it's merely one more reason you're reading this book.

I wish I could create a viral social media message made up of a dozen simple words: *God forgives you. Now, go find your people who do the same.*

Girlfriend, reread that message until you've memorized it frontward and backward.

You need female friends with whom you can vent and be real, friends who pray while picking you up off the floor. You need to find at least one sister who will adjust your crown with no judgment and whisper, "Settle down now. You are God's child. Hold your head high and keep a-truckin.'"

I won't lie to you, these women are hard to find, but when you do, hold on to them with every ounce of strength you can muster. Give thanks to God for these real deal women who are faithful to God, faithful to your privacy, and provide your heart with nourishment. And then, sweet one, you need to be that kind of friend as well. Remember those who fed your soul and return the favor. Oh, how we women need one another!

The second half of this book is dedicated to helping you get braver, smarter, and stronger. But before you can head in a victorious direction, you need to take this crucial step. With love and respect, I want to help you get rid of the shame you're most likely feeling.

Sister, you gotta bury the past and pray daily it doesn't sprout roots, for if it does, that's where the habits and addictions start to bloom.

It's only after putting the feelings of worthlessness behind you that you can get healthy and have fulfilling relationships with others, as well as yourself. It's time to take a seat and think through this. I'll wait. Go now and get in a quiet spot. You need some alone time.

This chapter is long for a reason. We cannot continue to walk toward the edge of a cliff, praying a passerby might give us a slight push.

You may have whispered to yourself the popular words of the apostle Paul, *"I want to do what is good, but I don't. I don't want to do what is wrong, but I do it anyway"* (Romans 7:19 NLT). Oh, friend, I, too, have looked into the mirror before, thinking that very thing. God put those words into Paul's heart, as He knew we'd need to be reminded that we're not alone in our struggle with temptation.

The enemy thrives on tempting our minds. We all have had sinful thoughts, whether we want to admit it or not. The battle lies in our strength not to act upon them. Of course, you already know that. Perhaps you're thinking like Paul, "I know what's right and what's wrong. I do. Yet somehow, I get tempted, cave in to it, and then I'm back at square one. I feel sick with shame that I don't have any more self-control than this."

I've been there, done that, and own the T-shirt. If you own that shirt too, then you're among friends. It's a constant struggle for anyone who inhales air on this good green earth. We are all trying, sometimes frantically, to resist that which tempts us. We crave a *sweet fix*, only to find it's not so sweet and comes close to decaying our sanity.

Deep down, we all yearn to develop into stronger women of faith. The struggle is between the temptation to be temporarily satisfied and the temptation to be an obedient child of God. Sheesh, the choice seems like a no-brainer. But it's not that easy, is it?

In Touch Ministries founder Charles Stanley wrote:

God knows Satan is working full-time to flood our ears, eyes, and minds with things that will sidetrack us. God will not judge us for those evil thoughts that dart through our minds, not even for those longings and desires that often accompany certain thoughts. On the contrary he sent his son to enable us to successfully deal with the onslaught of temptation. Temptation is not a sin; it is simply Satan's attempt to make us fall.[13]

As sisters in Christ determined to get healthy, please know this: Satan is aware of your plans and will be determined more

---

13. Charles Stanley, *Winning the War Within: Facing Trials, Temptations, and Inner Struggles* (Nashville, TN: Thomas Nelson, 2002).

than ever to tempt you and pull you away from God. Don't give in! But if you *do* give in, understand that God is still with you and loves you. So does this author, who totally knows you can rule over this! Hang on.

One of the enemy's favorite ways to keep you down on the floor, feeling absolutely worthless, is the main topic of this chapter: *Shame*. It's been around since the beginning of time. Adam and Eve disobeyed God by eating the fruit from the Tree of Knowledge of Good and Evil and experienced shame for the first time. (See Genesis 3:6–7.)

After realizing their transgression, they immediately felt self-conscious of their nakedness and tried to remove their shame by covering themselves with fig leaves. By hiding themselves, Adam and Eve assumed they were no longer able to receive God's love, grace, and mercy. *Their faith in God had changed to fear.* Can you relate?

So often we forget one very important truth: If we humbly ask, God is willing to give us His grace freely and abundantly. (See 2 Corinthians 9:8.) Reread that, sweet friend. It makes me want to go outside and scream a big "Thank You!" up to heaven, for this Southern girl has messed up a lot. But please know this: Freely and abundantly, because God sent His Son to die for our sins, we are forgiven. You, me—all of us. Over and over, we can go to Him. Run, walk, jog, or skip, He is there waiting to pick us up, dust us off, and whisper, "*I have you. Now, learn from this. Put on that armor I told you about. I'm going to help you along every step, even when you stumble. I am here.*"

Sometimes we may feel like that's too good to be true. Instead of basking in God's love and mercy, we quickly sink back into Adam and Eve mode and grab a fig leaf. In truth, shame is a potent combination of failure and pride. When we fall prey to our inherent weaknesses and sinful nature, we feel like we've failed our family, failed our friends, and have especially failed God. And good gracious, with the pressures on social media to at least *look* like we have the perfect body, the perfect kids, and the perfect life, failure of any kind is simply not an option. So what do we do when we feel like a failure?

We hide. We hide in our homes. We hide in hotel rooms. We hide behind social media and career facades. We hide behind Netflix or ESPN. We hide behind photo filters and costly brands. We hide at the casino, the liquor store, or the local pharmacy.

My friend, we have our own noontime well just like the Samaritan woman in the Bible.

Remember her? She was really good at hiding. She is never named, yet her encounter with Jesus is the longest one between the Messiah and any other individual in the Gospel of John. Traveling through Samaria with His disciples, He encountered her drawing water from the well. He asked her for a drink, and their talk took off from there—culminating in her salvation and many more from her town too.

We know a few facts about her. While her name is never revealed, we know she was a Samaritan, a race with whom Jews did not associate. We know she had had five husbands and was now with a sixth man who was not her husband. We also know, from understanding cultural traditions of that time, that women typically drew water in groups in the cool of the morning, and it was often a social occasion. The fact that she was drawing water alone, in the heat of the day, indicates she was a social outcast.

Because of her past and present, this woman lived with a constant feeling of shame. Yet after talking with Jesus, she discovered He already knew of her transgressions and still offered her living water to cleanse her soul and give her eternal life. She was in total amazement and ran to tell everyone she knew! But friend, I know that is easier said than done. It's hard to believe such forgiveness and love exist. To all of us struggling like the Samaritan woman, hiding from such a glorious fact seems to be easier.

Shame and fear of retribution start at a young age. When my daughters were young, our house seemed to have a revolving door, with sweet little pigtailed girls staying over on the weekends. Thinking back on those special years, our house was filled with giggles, spa facial concoctions, and single socks left behind with no owner. I sometimes wonder how I kept my sanity. I'll always remember one sweet ten-year-old who spent the night and constantly pilfered through the candy cannister. Without fail, every finger got covered with chocolate as a result of her enjoying our jar of chocolate peanut butter treats. My daughter later informed me that her friend was not allowed to have candy at home, so eating it at our house was a secret gratification. I felt terrible, praying we were not playing a role in harming her health. When the young girl's mother arrived to pick her up, I quickly apologized and explained that our candy jar had been the source of bad behavior.

I'm not sure which was worse: the angry look on the mother's face, or the shame on her daughter's. Thankfully, the child was not a diabetic, but the mother had a rule that sweets were not to be eaten. Sadly, she scolded her daughter in front of the others, causing the chocolate lover to sprint to their car in tears. She not only felt shame for what she'd done, she feared punishment from her mother, who was clearly upset. My daughter's friend later confided that she was worried she'd never be invited back to our home again. My heart broke into a million pieces for her. Although I knew it wasn't my place at the time, I wanted to scoop her up into my arms and whisper, "It's okay. It was just chocolate. You'll remember the next time. Just know you are always welcome here!"

That's exactly what God wants us to remember after falling victim to temptation. If we humbly ask for forgiveness, we are always welcome at His table. There is no need to cry and hide in the car, thinking you're an unwanted guest.

Sadly, as we get older, getting caught with our hand in the proverbial cookie or candy jar results in an even deeper sense of humiliation. It's at that critical juncture, when we drown ourselves in shame, that we are dangerously close to spiraling out of control. One minute of caving in to a temptation can turn into a habit and then a full-blown addiction.

CATHI'S STORY, PART ONE

Cathi, age sixty-five, was a widow who felt tempted to drink alcohol after her husband died. After attending an event with her sons and their families, she returned home and felt an overwhelming sense of loneliness. She began having a cocktail at dinner, enjoying how it made her feel. After a few weeks, Cathi began pouring more vodka into her drink and eventually preferred straight vodka. Soon, one drink turned into three. One evening, after running out of vodka, she decided to drive to the nearby liquor store to get more. After weaving on the highway, she was pulled over by the police, got arrested for drunk driving, and lost her driver's license. Having no choice but to call her son to post bail, she was overwhelmed with shame, knowing she'd embarrassed her family. "I felt like everyone stared at me in disgust," she says. "I finally decided to stay home and never go anywhere. My sons kept their distance and I missed my grandkids terribly. I started drinking more because I felt so horrible inside. I saw no way out."

Alcoholism among women is at an all-time high. And with that comes terrible feelings of hopelessness, as it is often a byproduct of shame. Whether accompanied by a denial of the addiction or an admission of guilt, when one feels they have nowhere to turn, their mind can send false signals that often result in self-harm. A downward spiral deeper into the addiction—or, sadly, suicide—is often the result of feelings of desperation.

The enemy is clever and has a cagey way of destroying our self-esteem. When we indulge in enticements dangled in front of us, he quickly changes roles, shifting from being the tempter to becoming the accuser and the condemner.

Remember, while shame pronounces us guilty and deficient, Jesus pronounces us not guilty and sufficient.

Post this reminder on your refrigerator if you must! The enemy hopes you'll skip over this reality and remain in hiding.

But today, you're going to look at things differently, aren't you? You know the truth. You know through God's Word and the death and resurrection of Jesus that His love and mercy are endless. Over and over and over. He's crazy about you! Girlfriend, you *do* need a place to hide. You just need to hide in the right place. There is nowhere else to go with your succumbing to temptation. You can try, of course. You may have already. Oh, I have been there. I've hidden in the places we've already discussed and have even created a few of my own. But we also know there's always a cracked door. Eventually, our weakness gets brought into the light, and it's there staring back at us.

Oh, but that's where Jesus also shines the brightest. He steps right into the light with you, whispering, *"I am right here, and I love you. I'm going to help you ignore the naysayers and give you strength over this. Don't listen to them. Listen to Me. I love you, and that's all that matters."*

Do you hear Him? Go to a private place and talk with Him. Then, sweet sister, wash your face, look into the mirror, and smile that beautiful smile of yours! Yes! You are a child of God, and He will equip you with the armor and strength you need to resist temptation. It may not happen overnight, but know this: you can do it without shame. Rather than remaining in the dark, you can celebrate your new knowledge of one incredulous fact: you are a child of the Most High King!

After a few months of secluding herself at home, Cathi told me about a transformative decision she made.

CATHI'S STORY, PART TWO

I stumbled out of bed one morning, looked into the mirror, and realized that not only did my skin look horrible, I felt even worse inside. My fancy moisturizer wasn't going to fix it. For some reason, it was then I felt God whispering, "What's it going to take? Isn't it time to get better reacquainted with Me and let Me love you?" I dusted off my Bible and began reading Romans. It wasn't long before I felt an enormous weight had been lifted. I invited one of my girlfriends over for dinner, told her I'd become an alcoholic and needed her help. She hugged me and said she'd help any way she could. Not only did she give me a ride to church, but she went with me to my first Alcoholics Anonymous meeting. It feels so good to live in the light and be real.

Yes! I pray that after reading this chapter, you realize there is no need to feel shame and embarrassment about your addiction. We are all sinful beings, and you are not alone. As a former teacher, here's your assignment: Acknowledge your addiction before God, praise Him for endless grace, and pray for strength.

It's one step at a time. It's not going to be easy, but please, sweet one, let go of the shame. *God will always take you back.* Oh, friend, listen to the song "Take You Back" by Jeremy Camp.[14] I've never met Jeremy Camp and doubt I'll ever have the pleasure, but if I do, I can promise this little blond will give him a Southern bear hug and whisper, "Thanks for the reminder, my talented friend, for I needed it more than you know."

---

14. Jeremy Camp, "Take You Back," on *Restored* (BEC, 2004).

I know, I know—it's one more song for you to listen to or download. You're welcome.

God is all faithful, waiting to take us back with open arms. When we steady our hearts on Him, lay down our shame at His feet, and trust Him with our life, we will be given a perfect peace. Write down this verse and keep it close to you:

> *The LORD himself goes before you and will be with you; he will never leave you nor forsake you. Do not be afraid; do not be discouraged.*   (Deuteronomy 31:8)

Remember Traci's story from the last chapter? She read this verse as well.

TRACI'S STORY, PART TWO

After talking with a therapist for months, Traci had finally learned to forgive herself for having the affair with Eric. Although she was sure others were still gossiping, she'd learned to ignore them and go forward. Sometimes, Traci still felt lonely and found herself scrolling through social media. One evening, a friend messaged her and appeared to be flirtatious. It was a sign Tracey's therapist had warned her about. Immediately, Traci decided to resist the temptation by closing her account. She was no longer interested in comparing herself to others and engaging in inappropriate conversations. Traci felt an inner strength she'd never known before and realized she didn't have to be in a relationship. She was just fine being on her own.

Traci remembered that the Lord was with her. He would not leave her or forsake her.

Yes! Like you, she was ready to quit playing the shame game. Now that it's behind you, let's figure out *why* we fall for temptations in the first place. It's important that we get to the bottom of this before coming up with a plan to put on the brakes.

Are you ready? You might want to turn on some music to get in the mood.

8

A GIRL'S GOT NEEDS

Now that feelings of shame are squarely in the rearview mirror, we need to figure out *why* we do what we do. *Why do we give in to temptation over and over? Why are we able to resist certain enticements, yet fall face first for others?*

In addition to knowing that the enemy is hard at work in tipping the scales, both therapists and pastors agree our struggle is also related to our...wait for it...

Our appetite.

Wouldn't you know that word would rise up again in the conversation? In this instance, it's not about watching carbs or counting calories. *It's about our feelings and our flesh.* Sure, I get frustrated when I see the stretched flesh on my thighs as a result of eating too many tortilla chips while writing this book. But the relationship between feelings and flesh is more serious than the number on our bathroom scale. It's about needs and the methods we use to meet them.

Besides the love of Christ, the love of my husband, and the love of my children, here are a few of my needs:

+ I need private time with a good cup of coffee. (With powdered creamer that doesn't make my coffee cold. Yes, I'm old school.)

+ I need a long hot bath in order to decompress at night.

+ I need my two lifelong besties on speed dial when I'm having a crisis.

+ I need to jam to some great music for a few minutes every day.

+ I need snuggle time with my ragdoll cat, Mr. Bingley.

+ I need to have my favorite lipstick and lip liner in my handbag at all times. (If they quit making it, I'll be seriously sad.)

Naturally, my very survival doesn't depend on some pinky nude lipstick. It may feel like it, but it doesn't. However, my vanity and the need to feel attractive—desires of the flesh—are tied to it for sure.

Friends, it's time for a heart to heart.

We need to take a closer look at our needs, how we go about satisfying them, and why in the world we make the choices we do. Some of our needs are very basic and God-authored, like food, clothing, and shelter. God created man in His own image, with intellect and emotions. He provides us with the ability to feel love, joy, and yes, even passion. He delights in us experiencing positive emotions because we are His children, and He seeks our heart. When we feel inner peace, we know our needs are in line with God.

Allow me to give you an example.

My sweet cowboy and I just returned from a museum show in which his amazing paintings were on display. Knowing I was stressed due to a family situation, he was determined to help me get my mind off of things. He planned every detail for a romantic weekend, complete with dinner at a swanky new restaurant. While I'm usually dressed in leggings and an oversized sweater, that Saturday night, I put on my black pants, black turtleneck, and my red leather jacket. Although part of me felt like a rocker in an '80s video, my sweetheart thought I looked sexy. Our candlelit conversation was sweet, the steak tender, and the dessert mouth-watering. The hotel we returned to was elegant and welcoming. It was a near-perfect weekend. Let's just say the food, shelter, and passion boxes were all checked. They were all in line with God, and we felt immense gratitude and peace.

If only life could always be that simple, when our basic needs are met, our desires are morally fulfilled, and we feel life is worthy of glowing reviews. But if you're reading this book, you're well aware that our needs and emotions can get skewed and run amuck. Let's start right from the beginning. Shall we say it all started with, you know...

Her.

It was all Eve's fault and her inability to make wise decisions. We've blamed every hardship on her at one time or one hundred. I cursed Eve's name during childbirth, as the contractions arrived too close together, and it was too late for an epidural. (I offered the doctor $500 for a Tylenol.) I shake my fist at her when a hot flash causes me to scream, "I'm melting, I'm melting!" at 3 a.m. (Send all thermal underwear donations to my frostbitten husband.)

But we really want to let Eve have it when we experience deep anguish. This type of pain, for sure, is a negative emotion that's a byproduct of sin and emotional temptation. Other ill-fallen emotions include fear, anger, lust, envy, and vengeance. Why? While God created us to experience emotions such as joy, love, and yes, even passion, the enemy tells us that those emotions are not sufficient to meet the need he places in our minds. Because of the existence of sin in this world, our needs get twisted, and the emotions are tied up within them. We end up in a knot so contorted that even Harry Houdini might not escape.

Remember our discussion about Princess Diana in chapter two? While biographers include details of her bulimia, illicit affairs, and outbursts with her royal in-laws, most of us can read between the lines: *she needed to feel loved.* That was the source of her pain. Sadly, the enemy whispered lies to her, insisting he knew the best way to satiate her desire to feel loved. Instead, she wound up on a cold marble floor, regurgitating food.

This need to be cared for and understood can also cause other negative feelings like insecurity, loneliness, and fear. As a result, we are tempted to seek out the easiest vice at our finger-tips to ease the emotional pain: alcohol and drug abuse, bulimia, and illicit affairs are but a few of them. Our clear thinking gets muddled, preventing us from grasping the serious ramifications of our poor choices.

Oh, but the enemy's whispers can turn into screams. Besides suggesting dangerous ways to satisfy our God-created needs, he gets super crafty. He creates a whole *new* set of needs that don't remotely resemble anything from God—the need for power, the need for wealth, the need to look popular, the need to look sexy and perfect online... He's creative, to say the least.

As a means to satisfy those appetites, Satan presents temptations of every kind, and we try out everything in his box filled with sparkles and sweets—lie, hide, exert vengeance, manipulate, participate in lewd acts... Our curiosity gets the better of us, and we wind up with broken hearts and stuck-tight addictions.

It reminds me of the first I time took a group of high school students to a dim sum restaurant. There were few authentic Chinese restaurants for them to try out in Appalachia. After raising the money to travel to New York City, I made it a point to take them to an establishment in Chinatown. Servers zoomed from table to table, pushing carts of steamed dumplings of every shape and size. My students' eyes widened as the servers removed the bamboo basket lids and instructed my group to pick out what they wanted. Soon, their plates were full, and the sampling began. Although they enjoyed the experience, it was only a few hours before their stomachs were rumbling once more. They yearned for a food they recognized—the familiar— to give them satisfaction.

While the enemy offers up empty choices that leave us yearning for more, God knows exactly how to satisfy our appetite: the love of Jesus. We will always be hungry and searching until we fill up our hearts with Him.

Curiosity is a powerful emotion for sure. It can get the better or worst of us. While our personality is developing, lots of factors come into play that affect our level of curiosity. Our education, religious background, our parents' hobbies or vices, and even our parents' work interests can affect our way of thinking. If you were rewarded for an experience during childhood, your interest as an adult is piqued further. Of course, that can be a positive consequence or a nightmare.

Mary Colter's curious streak was a blessing in disguise.

A daughter of Irish immigrants, Mary moved from state to state in 1869. Texas, Colorado, Pennsylvania, and Minnesota were a few of her parents' favorites, with the latter being one of the biggest influences on Mary. While big cultural advancements were evident in Saint Paul, Mary could not ignore the fact that thousands of Native Americans had been forced to leave in 1862. Mary's curiosity about their culture blossomed into a lifelong passion. Amazed at her daughter's artistic talent, Mary's mother found a way to send her to California to attend the California School of Design. After returning to St. Paul to teach drawing to high school and college students, Mary met a man who would change her life. Fred Harvey, like Mary, was intrigued by the Native American culture. He was constantly curious about the experiences that could be offered to anyone who longed to see the West. He knew tourists would need places to stay, eat, rest, and shop. Fred knew Mary could help him meet those needs.

As one of the first female architects, Mary Colter built structures along the Grand Canyon and completed twenty-one hotels (many known as Harvey Hotels), curio shops, and rest areas along the major Western railroads. The La Posada Hotel in Winslow, Arizona, and a large addition to the La Fonda Hotel in Santa Fe are two of her most popular designs. I've stayed at both and I must say, Mary Colter's architectural genius is evident in both adobe hotels. Although men called her an "incomprehensible women who rode around on horseback sketching designs," her profound curiosity transformed Western architecture.[15]

Curiosity can, however, lead one down a rabbit hole that is extremely dangerous.

Just ask Connie.

CONNIE'S STORY

After years of emotional abuse that ended in divorce when she was sixty-two years old, Connie yearned for a loving relationship. Filled with curiosity, she met a gentleman on the Internet one evening and knew he was special. James was handsome, charming with his words, and complimented her beauty. Their late-night talks went on for months, and soon, Connie fell in love with him. There was only one problem: James was a surgeon in the military, serving in the Middle East. However, he and Connie decided it was important for them to meet one another, face to face. It wasn't long before James informed Connie that he needed travel money, as his bank account did not work on the base. Determined to see her soulmate, Connie wired money to him repeatedly, and they made their plans. When James's online presence suddenly disappeared, Connie was absolutely heartbroken.

Sadly, I'm sure you can guess how this story ends. James was no more a surgeon in the military than I am a nuclear engineer. This con artist was operating what is commonly known as a catfishing scheme, a deceptive activity in which a person

15. Virginia L. Grattan, *Mary Colter: Builder Upon the Red Earth* (Grand Canyon, AZ: Grand Canyon Natural History Association, 1992).

creates a fake identity on social media, targeting an unsuspecting victim. Women like Connie who feel lonely and in need of love are prime targets for criminals like James or whatever his real name might be. Not only had he stolen Connie's heart, but he'd taken fifty thousand dollars from her bank account. The desperate need for affection, combined with emotional curiosity, can have tragic consequences.

The Internet takes advantage of our curiosity for everything from dating to impulse shopping. Ever noticed how after you've looked at an item on a shopping site, it suddenly pops up on other sites you're reading? Or when an intriguing news item pops up, it pulls you in with one click, dangling a carrot ever so slightly? Eventually, one click leads to another until it seems there's no way out? There's a reason it's called the World Wide Web. We have to keep watch on our curious character at all times. After all, it's what killed the cat.

According to most psychologists, curiosity presents itself differently based upon one's personality type. Isn't it amazing how different God made each of us? I am living proof He has a sense of humor. This Santa Fe hippie chick can be quirky one minute and a curious intellectual the next. Notice I used the word *curious* to describe a trait of my own personality.

American psychologist Lewis Goldberg theorized five primary personality traits that can be referenced by the acronym OCEAN.[16] This model launched thousands of explorations of personality within its framework.

---

16. Courtney E. Ackerman, "Big Five Personality Traits: The OCEAN Model Explained," *Positive Psychology*, June 23, 2017, positivepsychology.com/big-five-personality-theory.

As you read over the descriptions[17] below, consider which trait applies to you the most. Pay attention to each because there's a big question for you at the end. And keep in mind that you may identify with more than one trait.

1. Openness to Experience

This trait refers to one's willingness to try new things, think outside of the box, and be vulnerable to risk or pain. An individual with a high degree of openness is likely to be someone who has a love of learning, enjoys the arts, engages in a creative career or hobby, and likes meeting new people. An individual who is low in openness probably prefers routine over variety, sticks to what he or she knows, and is not drawn to abstract art and entertainment. Common attributes related to openness to experience include:

Imagination	Insightfulness	Varied interests
Originality	Daringness	Preference for variety
Cleverness	Creativity	Curiosity

2. Conscientiousness

Conscientiousness is a trait that can be described as the tendency to control impulses, set goals, and act in socially acceptable ways. Conscientious people excel in their ability to delay gratification, work within the rules, and plan and organize effectively. People high in conscientiousness are likely to be successful in their academic and work careers. People low in conscientiousness are more likely to procrastinate and be flighty, impetuous, and impulsive. Conscientiousness attributes include:

---

17. Ibid.

Persistence/	Ambition	Thoroughness/
Perseverance		Planning
Self-discipline	Consistency	Control
Reliability	Resourcefulness	Hard work

3. Extroversion

Most people are familiar with the concept of extroversion and introversion, which refers to how one interacts with others. In general, extroverts get energy from others or interacting with them, while introverts get tired from interacting with others and need to replenish their energy with solitude. People high in extroversion tend to seek out opportunities for social interaction, and they are often the *life of the party*. They are comfortable with others and are prone to action rather than contemplation. People low in extroversion are more likely to be people of few words who are quiet, introspective, reserved, and thoughtful. Extroversion attributes include:

Sociableness	Assertiveness	Outgoing nature
Talkativeness	Ability to be articulate	Fun-loving nature
Tendency for affection	Friendliness	Social confidence

4. Agreeableness

This trait concerns how well one gets along with others. While extroversion involves an outgoing nature, agreeableness concerns one's orientation to others and interacts with them. People high in agreeableness tend to be well-liked, respected, and sensitive to others' needs. They likely have few enemies, are affectionate to their friends and loved ones, and are sympathetic to the plights of strangers. People on the low end of the agreeableness spectrum are less likely to be trusted and liked by others. They tend to be callous, blunt, rude, ill-tempered, antagonistic, and sarcastic. Although not all people who are low in agreeableness are cruel or abrasive, they are not likely to leave others with a warm fuzzy feeling. Agreeableness attributes include:

Altruism	Humbleness	Patience
Moderation	Tact/Politeness	Loyalty
Unselfishness	Helpfulness	Sensitivity

5. Neuroticism

Neuroticism is not a factor of meanness or incompetence, but a level of one's confidence and being comfortable in one's own skin. Those high in neuroticism are generally prone to anxiety, sadness, worry, and low self-esteem. They may be temperamental or easily angered, and they tend to be self-conscious and unsure of themselves. Individuals who score on the low end of neuroticism are more likely to feel confident, sure of themselves, and adventurous. They may also be brave and unencumbered by worry or self-doubt. Neuroticism attributes include:

Awkwardness	Pessimism	Moodiness
Jealousy	Anxiety/Insecurity	Timidness
Self-criticism	Instability	Oversensitivity

DIFFERENT TYPES, DIFFERENT TEMPTATIONS

Now that you've read over the personality types, is there one that screams, "Yeah, that is *so* me!"? Which of these personality types do you suspect struggles the most with curiosity and temptation? If you're one of those women, then know you must be more guarded than other personality types.

Not long ago, I experienced in living color the difference in personality traits between myself and a close girlfriend. Sheila lives directly across the street and was the first friendly face I met after moving to Santa Fe. We're the same age, we hit it off from the start, and she and her husband have become two of the closest friends in our lives. I didn't think twice when asking if she'd like to run an errand with me to my favorite makeup store. "Sure, I'd love to go," Sheila cheerfully replied. "I need to get more of my cleanser and toner."

Allow me to point out that visiting a makeup store is one of my favorite outings. As an artist, I suppose I view it as one big art supply store. Upon entering, I immediately grew wide-eyed, ogling over the latest lipsticks, lotions, and liners. Although my objective was to purchase a particular mascara and eye liner, my brain whispered, "Ooh, look at that over there! Ooh, let's go down that aisle too!"

Sheila did not view this palace of potions the same way. She was finished looking in five minutes. She went straight to her aisle of choice, found the cleanser and toner she always uses, and quipped, "Okay, I'm ready whenever you are."

That, my friends, is proof of the differences in God's children.

If you haven't figured it out already, curiosity is a personality trait with which I greatly identify. While it has played a role in helping me fulfill some big dreams, it has also contributed to a few setbacks and disappointments. Curiosity is a trait that must be kept in check for sure.

Just ask my husband.

Regardless of who's doing the grocery shopping, whenever Valentine's Day candy is put on the shelves (in some places, it's before Christmas, but don't get me started), one of us usually purchases a small heart box for the fun of it. We enjoy a piece of chocolate after dinner, and that's usually enough. But what do you suppose Miss Angie does as soon as the box is placed on the kitchen counter?

Yes, you're 100 percent correct.

With great curiosity, I squish each one, searching for the beautiful milk chocolate piece filled with coconut. If I pick up a fruity cream by accident, it's a big yuck. I hide it in one of those brown crinkly wrappers. God bless my husband for putting up with me. He smiles and shakes his head. He has learned to like chocolate that looks as if it's been run over by a truck.

We all have specific wants and needs. Depending on the degree to which our heart is lacking, the hunger pains can be so great that we fall victim to unhealthy temptations of a wide variety.

In a nutshell: overcoming temptation is complicated, but it's doable with God's help. Stay on this journey with me, and you'll discover some healthy options to help you resist. I promise with this collection, they'll all bring flavorful success to your heart.

9

PATCHING UP WEAK SPOTS

You may recall from chapter one that a piñata was the inspiration behind this book. There's a very real analogy here. Whacking the sweet spot of a piñata is very much like what happens in our own lives. Like a big stick, triggers can hit us at our weakest spot, do a heapin' amount of damage, and cause us to give in to temptation time and again. But alas, whether we like it or not, our temptations, habits, or addictions finally get exposed for all the world to see.

SHELLY'S STORY

Shelly's plane touched down in her hometown, and she grew sick to her stomach. Although she could recall pleasant memories with extended family, Shelly couldn't ignore the painful memories that came flooding back: a critical mother, losing her best friend, marrying a man who cheated on her… She remembers hitting rock bottom and hanging out with the wrong people. Shelly wound up getting hooked *on cocaine and entered a treatment center. Now, twenty years later, she'd returned to take care of her dying mother. She felt as if she, too, was near death on the inside. Her mother was just as critical as ever with put-downs about her appearance. Within an hour of arrival, Shelly also ran into her ex-husband's new wife, who looked like a supermodel. It was almost too much to bear. Knowing she was coming back to town, one of Shelly's former friends messaged her to stop by, promising a good time and a way to help her forget about her problems. Shelly was home, along with all the triggers that had nearly destroyed her.*

Triggers are the enemy's finest tools to try to make us think he's in charge.

Ladies, it's time we pull on our cowgirl boots and kick these temptations to the curb. We must pray as we've never prayed before that our heavenly Father will equip us to recognize these dangerous triggers that entice our hearts and minds.

Shelly recognized her triggers. Thankfully, she'd been warned about them in rehab. Bad friends doing bad things would have transported her back to a bad place. She'd practice self-restraint and prayed herself out of feeling hungover, addicted, and morally broken. Shelly recognized the trigger and never returned her former friend's calls.

This chapter is all about weak spots and weaponry.

As Charles Spurgeon pointed out, "The flesh will seek to ensnare you and to prevent your pressing on to glory...Therefore, Christian, wear your shield close to your armor, and cry mightily to God so that by His Spirit you may endure to the end."[18]

---

18. Spurgeon, *Morning and Evening*, 307.

When I first moved from Kentucky to northern New Mexico, I was often alone, with my only constant companion being Mr. Bingley, my ragdoll cat. (My daughters are Jane Austen fans, so we had another cat named Mr. Darcy. Go figure.) One evening, Bingley and I heard sounds so terrifying that I was ready to call 911. It sounded like there was a woman in mourning who was wailing loudly somewhere outside. My heart raced, wondering if she was in pain, as it clearly could have been that too. My anxiety teetered on the brink, as her voice soon amplified around the entire back of the house. After calling my neighbor in a total panic, he laughed and explained what I'd been hearing. (I'm sure an eye roll was involved if I could have seen his face over the phone.)

Coyotes.

Duh. How was I to know? This writer had a lot to learn about the wilds of New Mexico. Allow me to explain. Most adobe homes don't have air conditioning, so screened windows are left open at night, allowing for the cool mountain air to pass through. This little luxury was lost on yours truly. I quickly discovered that if the coyotes made a kill on some unsuspecting rabbit or squirrel, it sounded as if hundreds of them were hiding away in the sagebrush, ready to pounce on any unsuspecting writer…er, person. They were usually far off in the distance, but goodness gracious, who wants to take the chance, right?

Needless to say, my nerves stayed on edge. One evening, I decided to google *coyotes* online. With a sigh of relief, I read that they rarely attack humans. But *rarely* was not the word I wanted to hear. I wanted an absolute, steel-clad assurance that these cackling varmints would never darken my door. Unfortunately, I found no such thing. The following advice was all I compiled.

HOW TO AVOID CONFLICT WITH COYOTES

+ Do not feed coyotes.

+ Do not let pets run loose.

+ Repellents or fencing may help.

Hmm. This looks like advice for kicking temptations to the curb, doesn't it? Don't feed the temptation, don't allow thoughts to run wild, and do whatever is necessary to repel and keep them at bay.

This chapter is a how-to list on following these three instructions. As I've mentioned previously, what we don't want, as Christian women, is for our temptations to turn into painful habits and, even worse, into addictions. It's exactly why I've written this book and why this chapter is so important. We don't want coyotes lurking around where they shouldn't be.

When researching temptations and speaking with women who have successfully overcome them, I hear one phrase more than most: *practice self-discipline*. This is the ability to control one's feelings and overcome one's weaknesses. We know it can be done with God's help, but we also know how easy this is varies from woman to woman.

As I mentioned previously, I was bullied at school. I was harassed for my weight and my acne. This may sound like a familiar story, but mine was a bit different. I was bullied because I was *skinny*. Mouthy girls would laugh at my skinny legs, especially when I wore my cheer uniform. I'd get sick to my stomach on the school bus, expecting words—or in one case, a giant soda—to be hurled toward my head. One afternoon, I flopped onto my bed and prayed, "God, You can make these girls stop if it's Your will. Perhaps You're trying to teach me something, but

I sure don't know what that might be. I love You, but right now, God, I don't like You very much."

It was terrible to say to my Savior, but tell that to a sixteen-year-old girl wearing a soda-stained sweater. On that same evening, I became determined to practice self-discipline on three levels: I was going to figure out how to gain weight, get my acne under control, and ignore the bullies. My mother began to make peanut butter and jelly sandwiches for me at night, to be washed down with a milkshake that included a raw egg. Like Rocky,[19] whose movies were all the rage back then, I was going to get tough. I got an appointment with a dermatologist, started a medication to reduce the cysts, and followed a strict facial cleansing regimen.

Any type of self-discipline, regardless of our age, requires visualizing the positive outcome as a result of our actions. In a few months, I'd gained a little weight, cleared up my skin, had my braces removed, and felt better about my physical appearance. It was my first foray into reaping the rewards of a little willpower.

As our Father, God knows His children must be taught. But the lesson He prepared for me at sixteen did not have the outcome for which I'd desperately prayed. Even though I felt better about my weight and appearance, something unfortunate occurred: *the mean girls were still mean.* Some of them were even worse. Although I'd exercised strict discipline to remove the excuses for their rude behavior, they simply came up with new ones: where I lived, the car I drove, the boy I dated—they grasped at anything and everything. But it wasn't until then that I realized one life lesson that has stuck with me: regardless of

19. *Rocky*, directed by John G. Avildsen (1976; United Artists).

how much self-discipline I exerted, there was always going to be someone or something lurking around the corner.

Life is not fair on this ill-fallen planet. Pain happens, and unfortunately, more is waiting just around the corner. We must learn how to cope in healthy ways; otherwise, it will poison us to the core.

From a psychological perspective, Dr. Ted Wiard explains our response to pain by using an interesting analogy. He says:

As we become an adult and mature, much like a blossoming tree, pain and loss start to occur in life: divorce, deaths, trauma, financial loss, etc. They're like seeds that get lodged deep into our soil. Unfortunately, if we don't learn how to cope with this pain, these seeds begin to sprout unhealthy weeds: porn, drug abuse, Internet addiction, controlling behaviors, etc. If we want our life to flourish, we have to create a bedrock and then rototill the soil. By getting healthy, we are adding nutrients to our life. We can grow the garden we choose, not the one that does nothing but grow weeds.

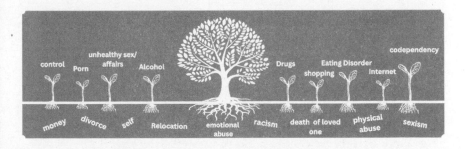

I just love this analogy. As a gardener, this explanation makes perfect sense. As a Christian woman, I know where to find this firm foundation. God is the rock on which I must build my life if I am going to grow in a healthy direction. I must roto-till my *soil* with prayer, building healthy relationships, and getting professional help if things get unmanageable. The next time you're working in your own garden, perhaps it's time to enrich your soil and do a little weeding.

Aside from these gardening tips, I promised to provide some actionable ways to help you resist temptation.

I'm a woman of my word.

MEDITATION

Neuroscientists and psychologists agree that there are several regions in our brain that carry out executive functions such as impulse control, a working memory, cognitive flexibility, and adaptability. In order to ensure that these functions work properly, there must be a healthy blood flow to these sections of the brain. One surefire way of doing that is through meditation by practicing breathing exercises, yoga, prayer, or whatever you do to achieve a quiet calm.

"Meditation has long-term benefits for certain organs, especially the brain," says Dr. Roxanne Sukol of Cleveland Clinic.[20] Increased blood circulation gets more oxygen and nutrients to every cell in your body, helping them to perform better. Getting that blood flowing can help you get through some of the stressful moments in your life, and that includes resisting harmful temptations.

20. "4 Meditation Myths, Busted," Cleveland Clinic, January 25, 2019, health. clevelandclinic.org/4-meditation-myths-busted.

When tempted to get online to watch pornography or engage in a secret chat, try meditating first. Breathe. Think about the ramifications of your behavior and how it will affect how you feel mentally and physically about your spouse or loved one.

If you're tempted to get on social media and have a relationship with someone online, go to a quiet place and meditate. Get the blood flowing to your brain and refrain from doing what you know is sinful behavior.

Breathe. Inhale. Exhale. I know you can do this. Once we're getting good blood flow to our brains, it's important we learn to recognize the triggers that tempt us.

REMOVING THE TRIGGERS

I started this chapter with a story about Shelly, who had learned what was *pushing her buttons*. Her mother's criticism and pain from Shelly's previous marriage were triggers that had once influenced Shelly into doing drugs. This time, she knew better. Although it was difficult, Shelly knew to use her willpower, practicing self-discipline. She didn't return her former friend's call, which would only have led to trouble. She also had learned to ignore her mother's hurtful words, reminding herself that just because her mother said cruel things didn't mean they were true.

When recognizing a potential trigger, you always have three choices: ignore it; cut off the relationship with it entirely; or allow it to do exactly what the enemy designed it to do—fire the weapon and cause an adverse reaction.

Think about dieting.

I know, I detest the word as well. If you're watching your carbohydrate intake, the last thing you want to do is drive by a doughnut shop with the words "fresh and warm" glowing out front. Their sign alone is a trigger. For me, the ice cream aisle is a no-go at the grocery store. (Chocolate chip coconut, you are *not* my friend!) When on a diet, avoidance of the trigger is the best form of self-discipline. But sure, it's easier said than done after a brutal day at work, when our child flunks a test, or things are so tense with a spouse that you can barely stand to sit in the same room. Stressed out, we tell ourselves it's not a sin to eat a delicious doughnut. It's just that if we eat too many, our thighs will pay for it later. It's easier to recognize triggers related to food since we see the result when we pull on a pair of jeans. (Yes, I hate it too.) But for many, the enemy will take a simple doughnut, twist it into a lie, and push us a bit further. Rather than admonishing ourselves for gaining weight, he knows which women to manipulate toward bulimia or anorexia. The enemy is always waiting in the shadows to trip us up in our high heels.

In addition to emotional triggers, such as the need to feel desired, other people can trigger us. For example, a woman tempted to engage in an affair might be friends with other women who've done so. By hanging out with others who condone such behavior, women are more likely to fall into temptation and engage in the sin.

The other participant in the affair is obviously a trigger too. He may whisper, "No one will know," "We're both unhappy and deserve to be with one another," or, "Let's just do this one time." *Lies, my friend. All lies.* Affairs never end well, reputations get destroyed, and children are often part of the carnage.

Of course, the enemy always tries to drown out these very real truths. Avoiding triggers is especially difficult if they're only a click away or sitting in an office down the hall. It will take extreme self-discipline, as we discussed previously, to remove yourself from their presence. Removing yourself from the situation may require you to switch jobs, change friends, or both.

It will be worth it, if at all possible, I promise. Listen to the words the Holy Spirit is whispering to you.

We can't proceed to the next form of weaponization until we look closer at one more dangerous prompt to remove from our lives. Disguised as the most innocent of feelings, it can knock us so far down that it takes God and all His heavenly angels to pick us up off the floor.

BOREDOM

Yes, this is a strange trigger, I know.

According to researchers at the University of Virginia, boredom is linked to mental illness and dysfunctional behaviors. In 2014, they placed a group of people in a room by themselves, with no distractions, for roughly six to fifteen minutes, letting them be alone in their thoughts. Thinking it would give their subjects the opportunity to slow down, sit quietly, and daydream, the research team was surprised to discover that many participants found the experience so unpleasant that they preferred physical pain. Sitting with a shock button nearby, 67 percent of men and 25 percent of women pressed it at least once to help them pass the time. Most reported they found it difficult to concentrate, and their minds wandered constantly.[21]

---

21. Timothy D. Wilson, et al., "Just think: the challenges of the disengaged mind," *Science*, July 4, 2014, www.ncbi.nlm.nih.gov/pmc/articles/PMC4330241.

I tried a version of this experiment when I was a sociology teacher. After overhearing my high school students complain about my class rules, saying I never gave them a break, I decided to shake things up. After they settled into their seats one morning, I decided to simply ignore them. (Don't worry, my principal had given me permission to act like a mad scientist for a few minutes.) Within five minutes, one student raised her hand and asked if I was going to start teaching. I replied, "No, not today," and proceeded to read a book. Ten more minutes went by and another student quipped, "Well, what are we supposed to do?" I ignored him. By that point, the students were in a state of bored bewilderment. After thirty minutes, things began to go off the rails. Four decided to throw paper wads at one another, three students went to sleep, and two tried sneaking out the door. Case closed.

Boredom can most definitely lead to reckless behavior. John Eastwood, a clinical psychologist at York University in Toronto, believes our culture's obsession with external sources of entertainment—such as TV, movies, the Internet, and video games—may also play a role in increasing boredom.[22] He believes that sensory overload denies us the ability to figure out where our passions and interests really lie. Rather than look within to determine those, we prefer to be told what they *should* be.

In one study of 156 addicts, the only reliable predictor of whether they stayed drug-free was whether they avoided boredom.[23] Prisoners in solitary confinement experience boredom that advances into depression, hallucinations, and psychosis.

---

22. Anna Gosline, "Bored to Death: Chronically Bored People Exhibit Higher Risk-Taking Behavior," *Scientific American*, February 26, 2007, www.scientificamerican.com/article/the-science-of-boredom.
23. Ibid.

Levels of self-harm and suicide are also common in intensely bored individuals.

You may be thinking, "But Angie, I'm not a prisoner in solitary confinement." Sweet friend, if you're struggling with temptation and feel no one understands, you probably feel very much like a prisoner.

Remember Susan's story in chapter seven? Retired, lonely, and bored at night, she waited until her husband was asleep so she could watch porn on her computer. Her husband watched sports until bedtime, and Susan usually wasn't sleepy then. She tearfully told me that their sex life had been over for years, and she didn't feel comfortable talking with him about their problems. Instead, she preferred to watch other people having sex.

What do you suppose is Susan's trigger? How would you remove that trigger based on what you've read thus far?

Aside from prayer, perhaps Susan should remove the trigger all together. She could learn a hobby, take a class, or fill up her time with a more meaningful activity. She could turn off her computer and phone at night, placing them in another room or even locking them up in her car. It sounds drastic, but extreme measures are often required when dealing with temptation. Above all, Susan needs to have a heart-to-heart talk with her husband, as well as a Father-daughter talk with God.

If you're trying to resist a particular temptation, ask yourself:

+ What is triggering me to do this?
+ What is the negative result when I fall into temptation?
+ Will it affect people I love?

✦ What is a positive health result when I don't give in?

Friends, regardless of the temptation in front of you, ask yourself these questions. And then, here's what to do next: *Wait two minutes.*

Yes, you read that correctly, and it's worth repeating. The next time you're tempted, give it a two-minute wait. We know the song and have it memorized, "The waiting is the hardest part."[24]

Resist the temptation for *two minutes*. Research shows it works. Try it. If it takes counting down every second on your watch, then do it. Whatever it takes. Heck, sing along with that famous song if you must!

Temptation occurs in all of us. Pastor Bruce Wilkinson states that whenever he's trying to resist temptation, the Holy Spirit often gives him the ability to resist and provides comfort to him in less than two minutes. He tries to control his emotional reactions and prays repeatedly, "Holy Spirit, You were given to me for comfort. I need comfort right now. Please comfort me."[25] Write that down, sweet sister. It's one worth remembering. Wait two minutes.

ACCOUNTABILITY PARTNER

Using an accountability partner—a person you can turn to for strength when you feel tempted—is another great weapon to add to your arsenal. In my research for this book, I found the comments by women over the age of forty to be interesting.

24. Tom Petty and the Heartbreakers, "The Waiting," on *Hard Promises* (Backstreet Records, 1981).
25. Bruce Wilkinson, *Overcoming Temptation: Break Away from Captivity and Embrace God's Freedom* (Eugene, OR: Harvest House Publishers, 2018).

While some praised God for having a friend they could call on the phone, day or night, others did not feel as comfortable. The latter made comments like, "I don't want anyone to know I'm struggling," and "I really don't have a friend I feel close enough to talk with."

I cannot stress this enough: there is incredible beauty in having a best friend with whom you can bare your heart.

My besties are two of the most important people in my life. They flew to New Mexico to be with me when my marriage fell apart, saying, "We'll stay as long as it takes." We can vent to one another—thank You, Jesus!—whenever a grown child has pushed us to our ever-lovin' limit. We celebrate milestones and put our heads together to conquer the obstacles that lie in our paths. My best friends are the super glue and puzzle solvers when life doesn't make sense.

Friend, you may need to step out of your comfort zone to find that female, but I promise it will be a decision you'll never regret.

PRAYER

I've saved the most important step for last. Prayer is the most powerful course of action before, during, and after our struggle with temptation. Besides the weapons we've amassed in this chapter, here are a few short prayers to help strengthen your heart and mind. Write these down, print them out, or come up with your own.

SHOPPING

Dear God, thank You for all You've provided me. You own the cattle on a thousand hills and the lilies in the fields. This is Your earth, and You've entrusted me to manage my part. God, when I am tempted to buy things I don't need, please strengthen me. Allow me to experience joy in moderation. Help me to use the money You've given me in a wise manner, and not to buy more things I don't need. Thank You for keeping me focused.

ALCOHOL AND DRUGS

Heavenly Father, I know You have the power to stop me from drinking or popping a pill. Help me realize what my actions are doing to my body, not to mention my family. If I am ever tempted again, help me remember that You are my healer and my defender! Do not allow me to take one more step onto the roller coaster of highs and lows. Take this from me and hold me tightly. I surrender this to You!

AFFAIRS

Holy Father, guard my heart and my mind. Convict me every time I'm tempted to engage in an emotional or sexual affair. You have given me sexuality and desires. Remind me to use them within moral boundaries. Guard me and do not allow me to go in the wrong direction. Please Father, do not allow me to sin against my very own body, a body that was created by You!

SOCIAL MEDIA

Dear Lord, You have created family and friends for me. Although social media allows me to stay in touch with community, it can tempt me in ways that it shouldn't. Stop me from relying on it too much. Help me overcome boredom, thinking I have to look at my phone all day long. Give me the wisdom to use my time more wisely.

Remind me to check in with You more than I check in with social media, for what You have to say is more important!

VANITY

Heavenly Father, thank You for breathing life into me. But in today's culture, I am overwhelmed with pressures to look a certain way, dress a certain way, or own certain things. Help me, oh Jesus, to realize that focusing on such things only leads to a feeling of inadequacy. I know You love me exactly as You created me. Give me strength to resist changing my facial appearances to the extreme. Remind me not to compare myself to others. Help me to see You as the model I should focus on. Thank You for loving me just as I am!

PORNOGRAPHY

Gracious God, guard my eyes. If I give in to the temptation of watching others have sex, please bring an emptiness upon me so great that I will never watch again. Break me from this bondage! Strengthen my resolve. Renew my relationship with my spouse so that I may enjoy pleasures greater than I've ever known before.

ARMOR UP!

I hope after reviewing these steel-plated suggestions, you feel cowgirled up with the necessary armor to shoot down the enemy. But may I stress an important fact without sounding too pushy? You gotta *use* these emotional weapons and not just look at them in the pages of this book. I know it's tempting, for lack of a better word, but you must be on guard at all times.

When Bill and I bought our house in Santa Fe, we were happy to know it had an alarm system. The real estate agent gave us the password, the contact information for the security company, and the locations of all of the sensors throughout our home. She reminded us, "Whenever there's an emergency, rest assured the paramedics or fire department will be there within ten minutes. It's an advantage to living in a neighborhood so well equipped. But remember, you must activate it when you go out the door." *My dear girlfriend, God installed a security system inside you.*

The manual for your internal security system is God's Word, and the password is J-E-S-U-S.

God knew we'd have emergency situations in our lives, including emotional ones involving temptation. Reread His manual, activate the alarm system, and keep your heart guarded.

Rejoice that His grace is there to put out the fire.

10

SWEET SATISFACTION

Runaway Bride[26] is one of my all-time favorite movies. Julia Roberts plays Maggie Carpenter, a hardware fix-it girl-turned-artist, who bolted at the altar on three different fiancés. This wasn't just a bad case of premarital jitters; this was abandoning the ship. Enter a curious news reporter, Ike, played by Richard Gere, who's determined to find out the true story. But that's when the movie gets really interesting. Ike begins interviewing the fiancés, trying to get to the bottom of Maggie's premarital trainwrecks. One particular question gives Ike the answer he's looking for: *"How does Maggie like her eggs?"*

Sounds crazy, doesn't it? But their replies were quite telling. The men say things like, "Scrambled, just like me," or "Poached, just like me." In every situation, Maggie liked her eggs exactly like her partner did. Due to her deep insecurity, she chose to enjoy whatever her fiancé wanted. After Ike confronted her with his discovery, Maggie tried to defend herself by saying, "That is

---

26. *Runaway Bride*, directed by Garry Marshall (1999; Paramount Pictures).

called changing your mind," to which Ike replied, "No, that's called not having a mind of your own."

Boom. Well said, Richard Gere. Every time I watch this movie, it reminds me of one blaring fact: *We can never love purely and passionately until we stop cheating on our true selves.*

May I make an observation here?

We may not have the big smile and bank account, but there's a whole lot of Maggie in many of us. Due to brutal insecurity, we are conditioned to be a good Christian girl and marry someone who tells us how we should like our eggs. These men usually have a presence so large that they take all of the oxygen out of the room. We end up feeling drowned to a depth so low we quit looking for air.

After treading water to the point of exhaustion, I too had to muster enough courage to come up for air and answer this egg question for myself. I won't lie to you—it was terrifying. But being shamed for having legitimate wants and needs is even scarier. If you are shaking your head or heart in agreement, know that I wrote this particular chapter especially for you. When I shared with female friends the topics that I planned to address in this book, I cannot tell you the number of women who looked at me with pleading eyes and emphatically said, "Angie, you gotta write about this. You simply *must*."

*So, sweet reader, how do **you** like your eggs?*

You may be wondering why this entire chapter is devoted to sexual temptation *and* satisfaction. It's because it is *needed*. It's no surprise that after interviewing and conducting research with hundreds of women, I discovered that struggles related to sexual needs and temptation were at the top of the list. It's also why this topic is mentioned in the Bible *187 times*—more than any temptation.

Before we get to all the beautiful means in which to achieve satisfaction, let's revisit one of the most popular sexual stories from the Bible that was *not* so beautiful: David and Bathsheba. I'm shocked that a steamy series about the affair hasn't yet streamed on television.

I'll give you a one-episode version.

Smitten by her beauty, King David summoned Bathsheba to his chambers, knowing full well she was the wife of Uriah, one of his elite soldiers. (See 2 Samuel 11.) Bathsheba later discovered she was pregnant and informed David, who was determined to cover up the sin. Calling her husband in from the battlefield, David hoped Uriah would sleep with Bathsheba, making it look as if the child was his. But here's where the plot thickens. Instead of obeying David's orders, Uriah slept in the quarters of the palace servants, refusing to enjoy a respite with his wife while his men on the battlefield were still in harm's way. Uriah did the same thing the next night as well, showing integrity in sharp contrast to David's lack thereof. It was then that David realized he must take matters into his own hands and concocted a more sinister plan: he commanded his military leader, Joab, to place Uriah on the front lines of battle and then to purposefully fall back from him. Uriah was exposed to enemy attack and killed in battle.

I'm sure you know the rest of the story. David and Bathsheba got married but, as we say in the South, they "endured a whole world of hurt." Their affair was made public, their infant son died, and calamities were cast upon David's family for generations.

Like David, our lives are filled with a range of human emotions. We celebrate on mountaintops and mourn in the valleys. But also like this shepherd boy who became king of Israel, we must lift our eyes up to our Maker and give Him praise. There's a reason why God called David a man after His own heart. (See 1 Samuel 13:14.) He humbly begged God for forgiveness and celebrated in knowing he was forgiven. David authored much of the book of Psalms; more importantly, he is part of the lineage of Jesus, who would be born over a thousand years later. Knowing all the wise and disastrous decisions David would make, God still chose him to be part of the royal blood line.

Oh, friend, I'm hoping you see a trend throughout this book. God chose *you*. Many of the people in the Bible whom He chose to lead and uplift are the ones who struggled, who were bewildered, and who felt they had nowhere to turn. Those stories are included to serve as a reminder that God has an incredible plan for each of us! *He will bring peace out of your pieces.* Knowing we are and will be always be sinners in one way or another, Jesus takes our sins upon Himself and says, "I love you anyway."

That, my sister, is the most perfect ending to any love story. Netflix will never top it. Pure love within the confines outlined by God is a very beautiful thing.

So is sex. Let's get back to the steamy topic of this chapter, shall we?

You may have given up on that feeling entirely. If you've been divorced, as I have, you may have been hurt, did your part in the hurting, or have firmly decided that a sexually intimate relationship is not in your future. Why would you dare want to stick your toe, not to mention any other body part, into the murky waters of emotions that might end up getting physical. Before you skip to the next chapter, I gently ask you to reconsider.

Sexual pleasure is a gift given by God, created for us to enjoy. It's exactly why we feel pleasure mentally and physically when having an orgasm. MRI scans show that different parts of the brain are deeply involved. These parts include the amygdala, hypothalamus, anterior cingulate cortex, and nucleus accumbens. Isn't God incredible?! Overall, there are about thirty active parts of the brain involved in an orgasm. During the height of a climax, the hormone oxytocin is released, causing a sense of trust and closeness with a partner. It's the very same hormone released when breastfeeding a baby, a powerful hormone that encourages a feeling of intimacy. Sex is also a natural painkiller, triggering the release of dopamine, the pleasure neurotransmitter, which also helps in reducing pain and stress. God creates a need in our bodies and designed us to satisfy that need in every way.

Sadly, while interviewing women for this book, I discovered that many Christian women are afraid to discuss their needs with their partners. However, most stated they knew exactly what their partner or spouse needs. "I know exactly what he wants," they often told me, rolling their eyes. "He wants the same thing as always and in the same position. It's the same ol' same ol.'"

Friend, I told you this is a raw and real book, and I'm going to disagree with you, if you're one of these women. If you've never asked your husband what he wants sexually, *even if you think you already know*, then that's on you. And likewise, if you've never stood up for yourself and told him what *you* need, then that's on you as well. I already know what you're thinking: "Wow, thanks a lot, Angie. You're telling me this is all *my* fault. Thanks, but no thanks."

Take a deep breath and hear me out. It doesn't take hundreds of years of research to know women are generally better communicators than men. In fact, women speak, on average, at a speed of 250 words a minute—about 30 percent more than their average male counterpart—and have around 10 percent more neurons in the area of the brain devoted to emotions and memory. This should be enough to convince you that you need to take the lead role as communicator. Don't gloat about it, even though we know you could. Just use it as an excuse to have a heart to heart with your guy.

If the ultimate goal is having pleasurable, incredible sex with your partner, then why not muster the courage to have a conversation? *Regardless of your age,* your relationship deserves it. You also need to be forewarned: don't expect your talk to go 100 percent as you planned it in your brain. We women tend to think we know how it all will play out. You may learn that your husband needs affection or stimulation in ways you never considered. He may find he'd forgotten that most women don't orgasm during penetration and need to be stimulated in other ways. *Keep an open mind and an open heart.* Reread this.

TIPS FOR SWEET SATISFACTION

This chapter is entitled "Sweet Satisfaction," which can be achieved in a variety of ways. Yet as we get older, some health conditions may cause us to question if sexual pleasure is still possible. Yes, you can still enjoy sex! But you may need to put a little more thought and planning into it than when you were younger. Remember, I promised to be upfront with you. Here are three big tips to keep in mind:

1. GET PHYSICALLY FIT

You may think of sex as leisurely, but you can work up quite a sweat during lovemaking. Exercise regularly. Nothing kills a mood faster than hurting your back or pulling a muscle.

+ Join a gym or work out at home. There are tons of free exercise videos online that you can use.

+ Exercise can release endorphins in your brain, which will improve your mood. You'll not only feel better after exercise, but sex will be more pleasurable.

+ Exercise also improves your body's appearance. Whether we like it or not, most men are physical creatures. While they will eventually see past our exterior and discover our real self inside, they are first attracted to what they see. Regular exercise can boost our sex life because it helps us look our best and feel confident.

+ We may also benefit from what's called Kegel exercise, which makes our pelvic floor muscles stronger. You can identify those muscles the next time you pee by stopping in midstream. You can practice tightening and relaxing those muscles several times a day.

2. KEEP IT INTERESTING: TRY SOMETHING NEW

This may be the hardest advice to embrace. But if you've been with the same partner for a long time, you may want to come up with ideas to add a little variety to your sex life. Again, this may be your responsibility, as men are often not as creative as women or simply unable to communicate it.

+ Wear something sexy. *There's nothing wrong with wanting to look sensual for your spouse.* It could be wearing anything from alluring lingerie to a beautiful outfit that your husband likes to see you in.

+ Change the time of day you have sex. If you're too sleepy at night, maybe sex in the morning is right for both of you.

+ Take it out of the bedroom and find a new place to make love.

+ Try different positions.

+ Shower or take a bath together.

+ Indulge in professional massages that will leave you both relaxed.

+ Visit an adult toy store or look online. Research popular toys that you or your partner can use together to improve stimulation. Sometimes lack of intimacy is a physical issue, and this can help.

3. TROUBLESHOOT YOUR MEDICATIONS

The side effects of some medicines can cause sexual problems. If you have reason to suspect that any of your prescriptions are dampening your sex life, talk with your doctor. Some that can do this include antidepressants, antihistamines, blood pressure *medicines*, cholesterol-lowering drugs, and ulcer *medications*.

AN IMPORTANT PHYSICAL REMINDER

After menopause, some women might have vaginal dryness that can make intercourse painful and can even result in tears and bleeding in the vagina. You may need to talk with your partner about more foreplay or try a silicone-based lubricant.

If you've worked through the big three steps above and are still not experiencing sexual satisfaction with your partner, you may need to seek the help of a licensed therapist. Of course, you can also pray that God will help you discover wonderful sexual intimacy with your spouse.

I'll be upfront with you: if you're working through these steps with frustration, the enemy may try to tempt you to seek sexual gratification in other ways. Engaging in an extramarital affair, exchanging sexually charged messages online, or viewing pornography are some of his favorite sinful tools. *Do not fall for this.* Go back and read the previous chapter. Adjust your armor and do not give up! Above all else, know that you are not alone.

Take satisfaction in that very sweet fact.

11

A GOOD CLEANSING

Girlfriend, it's hard to believe we're approaching the end of this book. It is my heartfelt prayer that above all else, you've come to the conclusion that God is crazy in love with you, even in the midst of your struggles. I have a hunch you're looking through your colorful bifocals and now viewing temptations for what they really are—artificial sweets in shiny packaging that will do nothing but rob you of joy.

You also know by now that I'm a straight shooter. God designed this author to speak out of both love and seriousness. I'm sorry, but you're sort of stuck with me. I cannot point this out too many times: we must cleanse ourselves of the fake sugar. Just like the hard candy that falls from a beaten-down piñata, once you taste the sweet, it's never as good as it looked. If we ingest too much, it will cause a cavity so deep within us that it results in some crippling pain.

I know about pain.

Girl, do I ever.

A few months ago, I had to see the one specialist whom I absolutely dread above all others. I mean, sister, I'd rather have a Pap smear or colonoscopy than endure the procedure circled in red on my calendar: *having my teeth cleaned at the dentist.*

I can't stand it. From the beep of an X-ray to the shrieking maniacal drill, the sounds are worse than nails down a chalkboard. My blood pressure goes up to the point where I once had to go to the emergency room afterward. I can't help it. It's how God wired me. I suppose I should be upfront and point out that my oldest daughter chose to become a dentist.

I know, right?

I've often wondered what I did as a parent to influence my sweet, innocent daughter to enjoy coming toward people's mouths with sharp instruments. As a child, she was always gleefully waiting in the car, happily anticipating her next orthodontist appointment. As she got older, I'd find her watching dental procedures on YouTube. I still don't understand it and have replayed my child-rearing practices over and over, seeking an explanation. But Kaitlin loves her job, and her patients love her. She sees dentistry as an important part of one's health, and I wholeheartedly agree.

I just hate when it plays a role in mine. I used COVID as an excuse for waiting too long between cleanings. After all, I was pretty positive I had no cavities since every tooth in my head is either sealed or filled. At age fifty-six, my poor teeth have endured just about everything. But upon opening my big mouth in the dental chair, the hygienist muffled behind her mask, "Angie, this cleaning is going to take a while, as you have a lot of plaque buildup that requires some scraping." Friend, *scraping* is not a word I like to hear, *ever*. I closed my eyes and sighed, "Can you just give me nitrous oxide to help me get through this?"

Surely, I hoped, fading off into neverland for an hour would chill me out a bit. To be honest, I was sort of looking forward to that part. But then she uttered words that will remain in my brain before I dare book my next appointment. "We don't use laughing gas here anymore."

Huh?!

It was worse than hearing about the toilet paper shortage at the supermarket. This simply could not be. Before I bolted out of the chair, prepared to burn rubber out of the parking lot, she mentioned she could apply pain relief gel under my gums, suggesting it might provide enough relief to get me through the harrowing ordeal. Knowing this cleaning could not be avoided any longer, I reluctantly agreed. *Girlfriend, it took forever, and it was painful.* In fact, it took two visits to clean them all. I'm not sure who hated it the most, me or my hygienist. By the end of the visit, she was sweating, and I was crying.

The memory of scraping, scaling—a word my daughter taught me—and the taste of that gritty tooth polish will be lodged in my brain forever. Those painful recollections will most likely cause terrified little me to whisper to myself, "It's just too painful. Stay away from that, Angie. Remember the pain you went through? Go have a facial or get a pedicure instead. Better yet, go shopping."

Isn't this what we also tell ourselves when facing tough hurdles, like avoiding temptations or kicking tough habits? Rather than own up to our actions—or, in my case, inaction—we get frustrated and scared. We come up with a zillion excuses to avoid having to come clean, excuse the pun. We yearn for an easy escape route to dull the pain, rather than making serious changes that would, in the end, make our life more rewarding than we ever imagined.

My sister, it is time for a good cleaning.

Just like my experience at the dreaded dentist, the longer we ignore the reality of our situation, the worse it gets. Whether it's unresolved abuse that influenced your decision-making, or being currently surrounded by a messed-up world that has its priorities out of whack, the source of your pain and anxiety can no longer be ignored. If you refuse to face the origin of the hurt, the result is an excruciating cleansing that takes years rather than months. It's time to subject yourself to this overdue purification. You'll not only feel better, but the others who care for you won't feel so darned exhausted from the trauma.

If I don't want every tooth in my head to rot out, I gotta do my part. Do I enjoy flossing, using a water pick, and going in for a cleaning every six months? Not really. But if I want to keep my pearly whites so that I can smile at my husband and laugh with my daughters, then you bet I will take care of my teeth. I will adopt new habits that are not only healthy for me but which benefit my family.

I will never get healthy if I'm unwilling to take the steps to get me there.

We have help, you know. God is the great physician. An appointment on one's calendar is not required. But we do have to put on our big girl panties and take the first step.

Before you utter, "Sure, Angie. You act as if cleaning up my act is as easy as flossing my teeth. Uh, not so much. I hate myself, and I hate the thoughts running through my head. You don't have a darn clue."

Oh, but I do, and I say this with all the love in the world.

I have walked in your shoes. I have stood alone with my thoughts, wondering why on earth I made such stupid decisions. I have berated myself senselessly for being weak, allowing inappropriate thoughts to course through my head. I have tried to make deals with God, promising to do better if He'd forgive me one last time.

Girlfriend, I get it.

It's tough taking one single step toward healing when we feel burdened and unworthy. Remember the chapter about shame? In case you've forgotten, allow me to introduce you to another one of God's daughters in the Gospel of Luke:

A woman in the crowd had suffered for twelve years with constant bleeding, and she could find no cure. Coming up behind Jesus, she touched the fringe of his robe. Immediately, the bleeding stopped. "Who touched me?" Jesus asked. Everyone denied it, and Peter said, "Master, this whole crowd is pressing up against you." But Jesus said, "Someone deliberately touched me, for I felt healing power go out from me." When the woman realized that she could not stay hidden, she began to tremble and fell to her knees in front of him. The whole crowd heard her explain why she had touched him and that she had been immediately healed. "Daughter," he said to her, "your faith has made you well. Go in peace." (Luke 8:43–48 NLT)

This woman knew about burdens and the need for cleaning. Keep in mind that some of the most beautiful lessons in the Bible come in the form of stories and parables. Praise God that the Gospel of Luke includes one about bleeding!

While most of us find it a nuisance for one week a month, this poor woman had been bleeding for what must have seemed like an eternity. In those days, bleeding outside the body, including the cleansing process of a menstrual cycle, was considered unclean or dirty. (Don't get me started on how it would have probably been accepted if it happened to men.) Can you imagine how stigmatized and desperate this sister in Christ must have felt?

Perhaps all women can. Perhaps it's why God had Luke include her in the Bible.

I can't tell you the number of times I've felt just like this woman—shamed, tired, beaten down, and feeling as if there's not another woman on earth who understands my situation.

Are you whispering, "Me too"?

You may not be physically bleeding like the woman in the crowd, but it sure seems that way. You may feel misunderstood, isolated, and scared just like her. You may feel past the point of saving, assuming you've caved in to temptation one too many times. You may have begged for healing, to feel the warm touch of Jesus upon you. Sweet friend, may I remind you of what Jesus called this woman who merely touched His garment for cleansing, who'd been suffering for twelve long years? He lovingly called her "daughter."

Let that sink deep into your heart. Reread it if you must. She asked, He cleansed, He provided relief, and He call her His. I'm so ever-lovin' thankful for this story.

Although there have been many times when I desperately reached for the hem of Jesus's garment, in one particular situation, I pleaded as His daughter *and* on behalf of my not-yet-born daughter.

Not knowing I was pregnant and because measles was on the rise in the early 1990s, I went to my local clinic and was vaccinated. Why I wasn't vaccinated for this deadly disease as a child is a bit complicated. Back in the 1960s, horse serum was used to create an antitoxin for diphtheria. But for some reason, my dear mother mistakenly thought horse serum was also used in the measles vaccine—and yours truly is allergic to horses. No shot for Miss Angie. But years later, when I discovered the truth and had the vaccine, I also discovered I was pregnant.

I went into a sheer panic.

As one who's always thrived on research, my brain went into hyperdrive. A live measles strain was coursing through my body at the same time my baby was trying to grow inside my womb. Upon discussing it with my physician and reading volumes of research, I realized the possible outcomes were not good. The potential of my baby being deaf or blind were at the top of the list. One physician even went so far as to recommend an abortion. Refusing to even fathom that option, I prayed like I had never done before.

As I got farther along in the pregnancy, my right kidney shut down, and I became severely ill. To make matters worse, upon doing an ultrasound, there appeared to be a large mass on my daughter's kidney or bowel area. My physician immediately suggested they induce labor, as my baby girl would need complex surgery upon delivery. My husband and I were terrified. We asked everyone we knew to pray for my daughter. I looked down at my belly with desperation, feeling as if there was not a single soul who understood my helplessness. So what did I do?

I closed my eyes and reached out for the hem of Jesus's garment.

Nine months pregnant, I barely made it down on one knee and pleaded for Him to hear my cry. I didn't care if I lived or died, but I prayed He'd give life to the baby inside of me. Two days later, I gave birth and heard my precious daughter take her first breath. I watched them whisk her away to conduct the necessary tests they'd warned she'd need immediately. In my heart, I not only touched the hem of Jesus's garment, but I grabbed it with every bit of lovin' strength I had.

Later that evening, my obstetrician came quietly into the room, along with the nurse wheeling in a bassinet carrying my baby.

"Angie, do you believe in miracles?" the doctor softly asked. "Because I think I just witnessed one. I saw the large spot on your daughter's abdomen during the ultrasound. My whole team saw it. We've just scanned your daughter from head to toe, and she's absolutely perfect."

Woman to woman, I cannot tell you the praises I lifted to the heavens. As I held my baby girl, tears of joy rolled down my face and onto her little pink cheeks. I had touched Jesus's garment. He not only heard His grown daughter's cries, but He delivered a baby daughter to her as well.

While there are parables and stories with happy endings this side of heaven, I realize there are situations in life that are soul crushing, causing us to question God. They leave us with a feeling that life's totally unfair and dirty, that a good cleansing or garment touching wouldn't even begin to touch the surface of our rage or deep depression. Chemotherapy, funerals, divorces, and overdoses are but a few reminders that our path on this earth is chock-full of detours and sinkholes, some so dark, we might think it's easier to be swallowed up and never heard from again.

So compared to struggles with temptation, habits, or addictions, we may feel as if God has more important matters to attend to. Praying for deliverance from a nasty habit, we tell ourselves, seems trivial compared to the trials others are facing.

But that couldn't be further from the truth. God yearns to hear from you, night or day. He is more than able to wrestle your struggles to the ground while managing the hurts of others. He longs to help His children and yearns to hear our cries for help. Whether you've hit a bump in the road or blown straight through the danger barricade, He is there to scoop you up and call you His daughter.

Oh, but we women can be stubborn, can't we? We simply cannot believe God wants to clean us up, especially if we plead to Him and hear only crickets. We stop praising through the storm and begin screaming at every lightning bolt in the sky. We get furious. We get tearful. We've done the hard work required—like putting on the armor and following the suggestions in this book—and when the battle gets too tough, we wonder why we're in the middle of a war in the first place.

Oh, how we love to argue with God. I've yelled so loud, it's a miracle I have a larynx left.

A year after my cousin Carolyn was diagnosed with ovarian cancer, she prepared to decorate our church at Christmastime. As in previous years, I often helped her, yet in that particular season, I was a bit surprised it was on her to-do list. Carolyn's system had been so weakened by chemotherapy that I assumed decorating was not part of her plan. Regardless of my concern, she insisted she was totally up for the task. With her boyfriend and I as her little elves, we pulled everything out of storage, taking note of what was needed, what was lacking, and what finally had to go to that big holiday trash heap in the sky. It took several days to accomplish the feat; mind you, it's a big church. Girlfriend, we went into a decorating frenzy so furious, it would put any decorating network star to shame. Forget the vacation movie with Christmas lights gone wild, we transformed our church into nothing short of a winter wonderland. It was taste-ful and beautiful.

And I was furious with God.

We could only work on placing the pots of poinsettias thirty minutes at a time. Decorating the giant Christmas tree took two hours instead of one. For each time we tried to decorate a section of the church, Carolyn would start sweating, get short of breath, and have no choice but to remove her wig and cool down for a while. It broke my heart into a million pieces. It made me so angry at God that I could barely contain my sanity.

Inwardly, I yelled at God. "How on earth could You dare allow this?! This woman is the most Christian woman I've ever known, and yet, of all people, You allow *her* to get ovarian cancer?! Are You kidding me?! This woman visits the children's cancer ward and distributes art supplies before having her own chemo. She is good, and she is faithful. Oh, and may I ask one more thing, God? Where are all of the healthy people who should be here decorating this place? Instead, here is this very sick woman lying in a church pew, letting her wig dry out? *Where* are the rest of Your people?!"

Trust me, this is the censored version of my angry prayer.

Unfortunately, my brain had drawn a total blank when it came to remembering what Carolyn had reminded me a zillion times: *God is good. It may not seem like it, but He is always always good.* I was so blinded by the injustice of the whole ordeal that I failed to see the joy Carolyn experienced while decorating her church. It was a form of worship for her. It also gave us time together that I'll cherish for the rest of my life.

God is good. It may not seem like it at the moment, but He is good and can remove the temptations or addictions that wreak havoc in your life.

But in order to experience a good cleaning of your mind, body, and spirit, it takes focus, and it takes hard work.

This here is that straight-shooter Angie I warned you about. God has given you the armor, but you gotta put it on, my friend. That's exactly why I'm encouraging you again in this chapter.

To help keep your mind and heart clean of all that tempts you, pray and try following the suggestions in the second half of this book. Think of them as something akin to the instructions on a shampoo bottle. *Wash. Rinse. Repeat.* It is a never-ending cleanup, but may I remind you of one thing? God sent His only Son to take on *all* of your dirty work. He gave Jesus specific instructions on the wash cycle you need. Now, press the *on* button and let Him fill you with His Spirit.

No spin cycle required.

12

A NERVOUS STOMACH

Before wrapping up our conversation, I can't help but address the elephant that's probably standing in your living room, threatening to squash all you've accomplished up to this point.

While you're now much braver in naming your temptations out loud, you may be feeling anxious about putting the second half of this book into action. I would not be surprised in the least if you're thinking, "Angie, I feel armed and ready to resist these cravings...but what if I get nervous and cave?"

Sweet friend, I understand. I asked myself this question countless times before getting to a healthy place in my life. Anxiety is ugly, especially when dealing with temptation. Not only does it play a role in our falling for quick fixes, but this condition makes us feel nervous about staying on a healthy path.

If you're a woman living in this topsy-turvy world, it's practically a given that you've experienced anxiety in one form or another. For some, it may present itself as butterflies in the stomach or brief heart palpitations. For others, anxiety is a serious disorder characterized by everything from panic attacks and nausea to binge-eating, headaches, and sleepless nights.

There's an ongoing debate on whether anxiety is genetically linked or a result of environmental factors. William R. Clark, professor emeritus of molecular, cell, and developmental biology at the University of California, Los Angeles, attributes it to both. Referencing studies conducted on both animals and humans, he found that while we all have serotonin, the neurotransmitter that mediates anxiety, we differ genetically in the ability of our brain's receptors to process it. He goes further to state that our environment also plays a role:

> Fear and anxiety are influenced by many genes; there is no such thing as a simple "fear" gene that is inherited from one generation to the next. The genes controlling neurotransmitters and their receptors are all present in several different forms in the general population. *The particular combinations of these different forms that we receive from our parents will predispose us to respond with greater or lesser degrees of anxiety to events in our environment.* But the degree to which our lives are affected by this inherited predisposition will depend to a very large extent on our individual histories—the number, strength, type and duration of events that elicit such reactions in the first place.[27] [Emphasis mine.]

Anna Bauer, a psychiatric epidemiologist at the University of North Carolina (UNC) School of Medicine, agrees. She

---

27. William R. Clark, "Is our tendency to experience fear and anxiety genetic?", *Scientific American*, March 6, 2000, www.scientificamerican.com/article/is-our-tendency-to-experi.

says, "We've seen time and time again in studies of families that anxiety does run in families. Children of parents who have a diagnosed anxiety disorder can be as much as seven times more likely to develop an anxious disorder themselves."[28]

UNC Health psychiatrist Anthony Zannas explains:

> What runs in families is the risk to develop these disorders, and then that risk is combined with an inciting environment...We are born with our genetic code, but the environment influences the extent to which those genes will get switched on or off.[29]

While we are not able to change our genetics, as adults, we can do something about our environment. For example, perhaps you had a mother who displayed a superstitious behavior like being afraid to celebrate good news for fear something bad would happen. Sadly, this is a common phobia, especially in Christians homes. I've met many parents who exhibit such behavior, which makes me incredibly sad. Not only do they warp their children's minds into thinking anxiety has some sort of protective quality, but they forget to teach them about the goodness of God, who wants our joy to be full.

If you grew up with this type of thinking, you have the ability to break this cycle. Rather than *live in fear of God, live in love with Him.* He adores you and is with you in your journey to overcome anxiety as well as temptation. While you cannot force a parent with anxiety disorder to get into therapy, *you* can choose how to tackle your own anxious thoughts.

28. "Does Anxiety Run in Families?", *UNC Health Talk*, August 11, 2020, healthtalk.unchealthcare.org/does-anxiety-run-in-families.
29. Ibid.

Just as important, I urge you to break this cycle before it influences your own children's way of thinking. Most scientists agree that molecular differences in our brains contribute to levels of anxiety, which is all the more reason to talk to a medical professional. Allow them to come up with a treatment plan for you. It may include medication, counseling, or both, but it is important to stick with it. I cannot emphasize this enough:

You are NOT less of a Christian because of your willingness to get the help you need.

Rest assured knowing this author is definitely cheering you on. I wrote this book as your friend who's been there and that includes suffering with anxiety. I've never lied to you, and I'm not about to start now. You may have to put up with a few naysayer comments like, "Counseling is for weak people," or "Pull yourself together, girl." *Bless their hearts.* I don't know which they need the most, prayer or pity, but they deserve both, I suppose.

Go forward. You're smart, you're capable, and you know God provided mental health professionals in your world for a reason.

As you get healthier, I cannot dust you off and head you in the right direction until I give you a few real-world tips of my own. They require some serious action, but if you can accomplish even half of them, you'll be less consumed by anxiety and on your way to feeling 100 percent in the moment!

SIMPLIFY CHOICES

Our brains are overwhelmed with information and choices at our fingertips. Naturally, it can contribute to feelings of being totally out of control. Clutter in every part of our lives can lead to both anxiety and procrastination. Here are a few steps you can take to simplify and declutter:

- Clear or organize your computer desktop

- Only allow snail mail to sit on your counter for two days at the most

- Remove clutter sitting on your counters or furniture. Create a bin and store those things that you don't need. You can always get them out later.

- Clear out your closet. Turn your hangers all the same way. After you wear a garment, put in back in your closet with the hanger facing the opposite way. After three months, look at what you've worn and let go of what you haven't worn.

- Clear your kitchen pantry. Get rid of what you don't need and donate to a food bank.

- If you need to shop for an item, don't go to a mall. Limit your choice to only a few stores. If you're online, remove your stored credit card information. You're less likely to go to a bunch of other websites if your info isn't stored.

TAKE A BREAK FROM SOCIAL MEDIA AND LIMIT COMPUTER/PHONE TIME

If you add up the time spent on your digital devices each day, you may find you have a closer relationship with the Internet than you do with your spouse or children.

- Create a realistic goal of how much time you should spend each day on your phone or computer, excluding reasonable work hours. Rather than spending that extra hour or two online, make a commitment to spend that time with your husband, connect with a friend, learn a new skill, meditate, pray, read your Bible, or exercise.

- Clear your inbox and spam folder. Do you really need to keep thousands of old emails?

- Lock your phone, iPad, or laptop up at night. Put it in your car or another room in the house.

- Take a sabbatical from all social media. Give your friends a heads-up that you just need to take a break. You may find you don't miss it at all. Don't allow others to pressure you back onto social media.

EVERYTHING IS NOT URGENT

Just because you can get information on your phone in a matter of seconds doesn't mean you should treat everything in life like a five-alarm fire. Think realistically about how quickly you really need to respond to an email or phone call. Whether in anger with a loved one or responding to a work-related email, replying too quickly often leads to regret.

LET GO OF PEOPLE WHO DRAIN YOU

We invest so much of ourselves in friendships, marriages, business partners, and family members. Letting go of painful relationships is hard, even if it's holding us back from being our true selves. While you can't just abandon family members, you can protect your mental health by putting up boundaries and communicating those boundaries to those involved. Regardless the type of relationship, it's time to part ways if the following types of discord are present:

+ Verbal, emotional, or physical abuse

+ Consistent dishonesty or disloyalty

+ Constant negativity

+ Harmfully irresponsible

+ Refusal to get treatment for mental issues or addiction

+ Doing all the taking in the relationship and never giving or making investments in *you*. Remember, it takes two willing people to make a friendship or relationship work.

You can't build a relationship with someone if they're not willing to help carry the bricks.

STOP LISTENING TO FAKE NEWS

I realize this is a touchy subject. It's easy to get pulled into a constant loop of anxiety if you do nothing but listen to false sentiments whirling around you. Different media outlets present their own doom and gloom angles of the world, contributing to feelings of anger and deep frustration. Have mercy! This country has never been more divided. But make no mistake, regardless of your political views, both sides have played a role and profited large sums of money in the process. While you're sure to find some show that aligns with your way of thinking, before you decide what's fake and what isn't, might I suggest that you listen to *both* sides of a news item before jumping to conclusions?

That's exactly what my husband and I try to do. Then we simply grab the remote and turn the TV off. God gave us a brain to arrive at our own conclusions. We'd go crazy if we left the TV tuned to one channel all day long, allowing the constant harping to bore into our subconscious. Most of our parents tuned in for thirty minutes to watch the evening news. That was it. We need to do the same and then turn it all over to God.

NO QUICK FIX

Trust me, I realize this punch list can't be accomplished overnight. But committing yourself to putting a dent in each one can have life-changing consequences. You'll not only have a heathier outlook for your future, but you'll be more present for your loved ones. You have the power to accomplish all of the steps I've just mentioned. Whenever you doubt yourself and your strength, go to Psalm 51:12: *"Restore to me the joy of your salvation and grant me a willing spirit, to sustain me."*

I love how Pastor Bryan Hallmark elaborates on this verse:

On those times when we feel we've disappointed both God and ourselves, we must not only repent, but we should ask God to restore us. *Repentance* is all about us asking for mercy and forgiveness from God. *Restoration* is about us asking for joy within God. We need both to be at peace.[30]

Isn't that such a wonderful reminder? The same power that raised Jesus from the grave is in *you*. The. Same. Power. He can restore a peace within you that defies understanding. The

---

30. Pastor Bryan Hallmark, "Putting God First," Christian Life Church, Santa Fe, NM, January 1, 2023.

awesomeness God placed within you can squash any feelings you may have of being out of control.

In essence, you need an escape ramp.

Although we have ski areas in northern New Mexico, many enjoy traveling a few hours north to Wolf Creek in southern Colorado. Known as having the most snow in the state, it features over a hundred trails for any powder hound who wishes to traverse. Whether gliding down green slopes (easy) or black diamond slopes (difficult), the views over the Rio Grande National Forest are stunning. Sitting atop a ski lift is one of my most favorite means of viewing God's majesty.

But don't utter those words to a truck driver.

With stretches as wide as four lanes, U.S. Route 160 at Wolf Creek Pass can deceive drivers into thinking there is ample room to navigate it. Adding high speeds to this miscalculation creates dangerous conditions, particularly for commercial vehicle drivers. It doesn't take but a few seconds for a truck's brakes to get overheated and fail. The driver forgets about the steep grade, loses complete control, and puts his life and the lives of other drivers in jeopardy. If the truck is overloaded, the extra weight causes it to zoom even faster toward possible destruction.

That's why the highway department created an escape or runaway ramp. Covered with sand, gravel, or wire nets, truck drivers can steer their vehicle onto the ramp in hopes of slowing down its momentum. The highway officials remind drivers that there is no charge for using the ramp, and they should call 911 if they need further assistance.

The next time you feel anxious or out of control, use the escape ramp God provided for you. There's no need to call 911;

just call upon the name of Jesus. It happens to all of us, for we forget just how treacherous this road of life can be. Close to caving in to a temptation, we tell ourselves we've got it all under control. But that's often when the stressors get too great, and it's too late to turn around. Go back and read the suggestions in this chapter. Then, my beloved friend, remain calm and use Jesus as your escape ramp. He will provide the grace and safety you need at a moment's notice. You can let off the brakes now. He never fails.

He's got you.

13

YOUR GUEST LIST FOR THE PARTY

I love parties.

I love the preparation almost as much as the party itself. What can I say? I'm a bit of a planner. But sometimes I have grandiose ideas that don't quite materialize as I'd planned.

The first year I moved to Santa Fe, I had the wackadoodle idea of making peanut butter roll for all of my neighbors at Christmastime. Never heard of this dessert? Well, my sugar-loving friend, you have missed out. Peanut butter roll is a heavenly confection of light-as-air fondant rolled up as a pinwheel with creamy peanut butter. One bite of this sugary swirl, and you'll think you've fallen straight into the arms of Jesus. *It is that good.*

Okay, okay, maybe I'm exaggerating a tiny bit. Perhaps part of the reason peanut butter roll is so mind-blowingly delicious is because of one small fact I should mention: making it is not for the faint of heart. I'm not sure where my favorite candy gets its origin, as I have never seen it made or sold outside of the state of Kentucky. Growing up there, my family always had a roll of it for Christmas—and that was *only* because our neighbor, Ann, had perfected the recipe. I mean, ladies, this woman knew her way around a peanut butter roll. My dad waited all year to cut the first slice off the glorious white log of goodness. The spirals were so perfect, they looked as if they should be in a Savannah candy shop.

I'd like to have a dollar for every woman in Kentucky who has tried to make peanut butter roll and failed. This little author would be sitting pretty.

The high altitude of Santa Fe must have rendered me loony when I made the decision to try making this candy for friends. Clearly, I had a bout of amnesia, for I had forgotten that I'd never made it successfully after twenty years of trying. Yeah, you read that correctly. One year, I blew up a mixer. Another year, the fondant got hard as a brick. Once, I even tried to convince my daughters it was perfect as a gooey ice cream topping. They didn't buy it. It was terrible.

But post-pandemic, there was something about my jovial attitude that convinced me I could master the recipe. I sent Bill to the grocery story with a honey-do list. Soon, my kitchen workspace was as organized as an operating room. I was armed with more sugar than Russell Stover. I'd gone over the recipe a thousand times. While I worked my sweet magic in the kitchen, Bill painted in his studio, periodically checking to see if I was still alive. After an hour of trying, I decided to wave the white flag.

Peanut Butter Roll: 1; Angie: 0.

I wanted to cry. It was way too flimsy.

I decided to try it again.

Peanut Butter Roll: 2; Angie: 0.

The trash got heavy, and I became heavy-hearted.

That's when I heard from the peanut gallery. "Why don't you call Kim?" my darling husband suggested. "I'm not trying to rub it in, honey, but she knows how to make it. Perhaps you can Facetime her while you're making it, and she'll guide you."

I put my knife back into the drawer and realized he was probably correct. I called Kim and she guided me through the mixing part, which had given me the most trouble.

Peanut Butter Roll: 2; **Angie: 1!**

Oh yeah, baby!!! It would never make the cover of *Taste of Home* magazine, but it was sliceable, and it was gooood. (I may or may not have this herculean feat on video.) Thank God for friends. I couldn't have done it without my best friend. Kim coached me over the phone, laughed at the powdered sugar in my hair, and cheered when I was finally victorious in the kitchen. Here's our recipe, for what it's worth.

PEANUT BUTTER ROLL

(*A sweet temptation you're allowed to enjoy*)

Ingredients

4 cups white sugar
1/2 cup white corn syrup
1 1/4 cup water
4 egg whites
1 tbl. butter
1/4 cup powdered sugar
1/3 cup peanut butter

Directions

Boil sugar, corn syrup, and water until the hard ball stage (250 degrees) using a candy thermometer. Remove from heat and set aside to cool for 5-10 minutes.

While mixture is cooling, beat 4 egg whites until they are fairly stiff. *Slowly* pour hot mixture into the egg whites and whip mixture until it loses its gloss. ***This takes forever, at least 25 minutes.*** It's best to use a stand mixer; otherwise, you'll blow up a hand mixer or will sprain your hand trying to beat this stuff to death.

Pour mixture onto a buttered wax paper that's been sprinkled with powdered sugar. Roll out into rectangle 1/4" thick and spread a thin layer of peanut butter over the entire top. Roll into a log and cover with plastic wrap. Chill for a couple hours and then slice.

Good luck! I hope you are victorious on your first attempt... and if so, please don't rub it in. Just savor every bite.

This is a long way around to remind you of the importance of a guest list.

If you're at the point in this book where you've begun putting my suggestions into action, I hope to heaven you feel my giant high five coming off the page! I am spinning around, praising God that you're reading this book and feeling better about yourself and your Savior. YES! I am tickled pink that you've been peeling back the layers of hurt and taking big girl steps toward healing. You're now better at recognizing those *fake sugars* that lead to nothing but pain and regret.

You deserve to P-A-R-T-Y with the people on your guest list. As you grow stronger in becoming a woman of resolve, I can't stress enough the importance of surrounding yourself with women who have your back.

I like to call them your *sister circle*.

Pastor Louie Giglio says, "When a harmful thought or temptation comes into our minds, we have a choice. We can either discard that thought or entertain it. If we discard it, good. But if we entertain it, that's when the Devil sits at our table."[31]

Who sits with you at the table of grace, reminding the enemy he's no longer welcome? Who is your plus one, two, or three, celebrating that God sacrificed His Son so you can smile and laugh in freedom?

Who are your people?

Let me be clear, I'm not talking about your biological family, although some of them may be included *only* if they positively feed your soul. I'm talking about *your people*. Those people you get to choose. Those who believe in you and make sure you know it. Those who smile when you walk into a room. Those who sense when you're struggling and send you a text saying, "Young lady, it's time we meet for lunch and have a looooong talk. I got you, sister. I got you."

If you aren't sure who's in your sister circle, then it's time you figure that out.

Let's start by asking yourself a few questions. *Note: you cannot include your spouse and I'll get to that later.*

---

31. Louie Giglio, *Don't Give the Enemy a Seat at Your Table*, Study Guide edition (Nashville, TN: Harper Christian Resources, 2022).

+ If you were to get sick and need to be taken to the hospital, who could you count on to drive you there?

+ If you just received an answer to a long-standing prayer, who do you tell first, thanking them for praying for you?

+ If you need to laugh and get in a better mood, who do you call?

+ If you have a secret to confess that you know will be taken to the grave, who do you tell?

+ Who knows exactly what to say or what not to say when you're having a meltdown?

+ If you're having issues with a family member and need some objective advice, who do you call?

If you have answers to each of these questions, then may I introduce you to your sister circle. Some of these women may have more than one role, and that's perfectly okay. They may not even know one another well. They don't even have to live in the same town or state. A few women in my circle live in Santa Fe, and a few reside in other states. But they all have one thing in common: they all love me, and I love them. We uplift, forgive, cry, push back, and giggle until our sides hurt. We pray for one another, and when it's needed, we may send a text that simply says, "I am here for you."

There's also one good reason I prefaced the quiz by saying your spouse cannot be the answer to any of the questions. He lacks a key feature that the rest of your circle possesses:

Two X chromosomes. He's not a woman.

Although you may consider him your lover, soulmate and knight in shining armor, your guy is not a female who understands the varied emotions, worries, and health scares that are unique only to us. He's never had a period or a night sweat. He's never had breasts pressed into pancakes during a mammogram. He's never stood by an exit door, hoping a Southern gentleman would open it with a smile. (I am soooo not ashamed to need that.)

It's going to be hard for your husband to be objective, regardless of what you tell yourself. He lives under the same roof with you and sleeps by your side. He may worry about the repercussions of giving his opinion on a matter he knows could affect the most important relationship in his life. Don't do that to him. Don't do that to you.

It's tough being a woman, and it's not the same as being a man. It's why you need a sister circle.

And not to lay down too many ground rules, but this circle should not include an adult daughter either. You're her mother, and while it's an absolute blessing to have an adult daughter as your friend, she doesn't need the added responsibility of being in a circle of women who have issues she's yet to experience. Although she may insist on her ability to be an objective listener, it's subconsciously difficult. She is all too aware you've provided unconditional love her entire life, not to mention you were the sole person responsible in keeping her alive for nine months. Don't put that kind of pressure on your sweet daughter.

Perhaps you're thinking these two rules narrow down your list a bit. Perhaps up until now, you've told yourself you don't really need a sister circle, as the world has definitely sent us the message we're perfectly fine on our own. We can work from home, shop from home, and have groceries delivered to the front door. We can watch YouTube and learn how to give ourselves everything from a haircut to a pedicure. We can pay our bills and even get a college degree online. And sadly, we can have emotional and sexual relationships online and assume that it's perfectly healthy.

My friend, that simply is not so.

The statistics prove it. While we have the ability to be more self-sustaining than ever before, depression, anxiety, and suicide rates have never been higher. Why? Because God designed us to be social beings. We need one another. We need hugs and real physical intimacy. We need to look into each other's eyes and be able to say, "I love you." We need other people.

You need sisters in your circle.

I just returned from a girls' trip to Maine. Each year, my two best friends of over thirty years choose a place to explore in the U.S. Since they live in Kentucky and I live in New Mexico, they often come out West, but this year, we decided to do it lobster style. Decked out in our "Girl's Trip 2022" shirts, we ventured up and down the coast of Maine. We cried with laughter over cocktails. We sighed with worry, wondering if our adult daughters were making wise decisions. We offered one another advice on healthcare for our aging parents. We shopped till we dropped at the Freeport outlets. I went up a jeans size thanks to an overdose of lobster tails and blueberry pie. It was worth every extra calorie to experience it with key members of my sister circle.

If you're having trouble forming your circle, know that it's perfectly normal. While some women have more free time to meet friends over a mutual hobby, some women prefer to keep to themselves. It's easy to stay inside and read a book or come straight home from work and lock the door. Some women have been too busy raising children and grandchildren to worry about a circle of women. Life gets complicated. Understood.

But no more excuses. It's time to get out of your comfort zone. Invite a friend to lunch and learn more about them. Text a new acquaintance and break the ice by sending a new recipe or funny joke. Join a gym and make a conscious effort to introduce yourself to another woman. Put yourself out there and take the risk.

Keep in mind that if you want real deal friends, you need to be the real deal friend in return. Sure, we all have friends who are fun to go to dinner with or laugh over a glass of wine, but what do you really *know* about them? Do they share with you or do you do all the sharing? Have you ever gently asked them why that may be? Perhaps it's time for a conversation. Perhaps she's putting up a wall because she's struggling with her own demons.

Your sister circle should feed your soul, and my friend, *we all need to be fed*. For if our soul starts to starve, the enemy will rush in and try to feed it garbage. He longs to keep you alone in the corner, gorging on harmful temptations. And just like that famous movie quote, "Nobody puts Baby in a corner!"[32] Remember that.

Go put on your sparkly dress and celebrate! You're about to form a gorgeous support system that will have your back, 24/7. It's time to party with your sisters at the table of grace.

---

32. *Dirty Dancing*, directed by Emile Ardolino (1987; Vestron Pictures).

EPILOGUE

Okay, I'll admit I'm a little sad. I feel like I'm saying goodbye to a friend, but I'm convinced our paths will cross again.

We started on this journey feeling much like a piñata. After a tough break, we stopped the spinning and had no choice but to look at the jagged pieces of our lives scattered on the floor. Although it was painful, we removed the shiny wrappers and called the temptations out for what they are—tasteless and harmful to our relationship with God, our family, and ourselves.

You are a warrior. You've wrestled dangerous cravings to the ground.

If these temptations whisper to you again, you have the armor and cowgirl boots to kick them straight to the curb. Oh, my friend, I am so proud of how far you've come. Above all, it is my overwhelming prayer that you've decided to walk away from the shame and instead run with reckless abandon into the light of God's grace. Get to know His Son, Jesus. Ask Him into your heart, and you will feel a warmth that will sustain you for the rest of your life.

I've never lied to you and don't intend to start now, so I must mention that there will be times in your life when you feel a chill. You may feel so cold and far from Jesus that you're tempted to warm yourself by a fire that will do nothing but singe your sanity and burn your self-worth.

Don't go there.

Instead, grab a blanket, have some alone time, and focus on the second half of this book. Go back to God's Word and reread about His daughters. Refamiliarize yourself with the woman at the well. Touch Jesus's garment like the woman in Luke. *Jesus loved them just as He adores you.*

Pray. Breathe. Wait two minutes before acting hastily. Call your accountability partner. Consult with your physician or counselor. Remove yourself from the temptation or tempters and lean in hard on your sister circle. Look in the mirror and remind yourself who you really are: *You are God's daughter.* Write it in lipstick on your bathroom mirror if you must.

In my times of pain and uncertainty, I often repeat a wise reminder from Max Lucado:

> You'll get through this. It won't be painless. It won't be quick. But God will use this mess for good. In the meantime, don't be foolish or naïve. But don't despair either. With God's help you will get through this.[33]

You will get through this. I just know it.

---

33. Max Lucado, *You'll Get Through This: Hope and Help for Your Turbulent Times* (Nashville, TN: Thomas Nelson, 2013.)

Before writing this heartfelt farewell, I had my morning prayer, followed up with a cup of coffee while applying my makeup and watching my favorite morning show. (We women are multitaskers to a fault.) My favorite segment always involves the hosts pulling a few women from the crowd and granting them a complete makeover. These women are often chosen because they're holding an attention-grabbing sign that shouts, "Pick Me!" or they've had a family member write a letter explaining why they deserve a gift of transformation.

Once the ladies are chosen, they are whisked away and instructed to let the professionals do their thing. New makeup? Check. Flattering outfit? Check. Sexy hairstyle and color? Check. Check.

I suppose I should also point out that the lucky winner is blindfolded during the entire process. She's prevented from seeing the outcome until every person working on her has completed their task. The transformation always elicits the same response: when the blindfold is removed, the woman is brought to tears, amazed at her reflection in the mirror. A few loved ones are usually there cheering, startled at the like-new woman standing before them.

Feel familiar? Haven't you just experienced the same?

Before now, it was hard to see or understand what was going on in your life. You called out to God, "Here I am—pick me!" You allowed Him to give you strength, went through the necessary steps to get healthy, and now, my sweet friend, you've been made new. Your weak spots have been patched, and there's barely a scar. Stand in front of the mirror and smile like you've never smiled before!

In your heart of hearts, you knew all along that Jesus was the only one qualified to perform this extraordinary transformation. He ever so gently removed your sugarcoated tendencies, placed healthy cravings inside of you, and exposed to the world the beautiful woman you are—smarter, stronger, and hungry for food that's truly delicious and good for you: God and His Word.

Now, sweet sister, fill up your plate and enjoy every flavor.

ABOUT THE AUTHOR

Angie Haskell is an award-winning author, artist, and speaker who engages audiences with her approachable personality, Southern charm, and passion for helping women form healthy relationships with themselves and others.

Angie has worn many hats with great enthusiasm. She is the author of several books for children and young adults (under the name Angie Spady): *The Channing O'Banning* Series and *The Desperate Diva Diaries,* now in three languages. As a high school teacher, she was featured on PBS as well as *Kentucky Teacher* magazine for her innovative teaching techniques. Her paintings are featured in esteemed art galleries in Jackson Hole, Wyoming; Santa Fe, New Mexico; and Tucson, Arizona. She reminds herself and all women that God created us to survive and thrive.

A native of Kentucky, Angie is a woman of deep faith who survived the death of her two best friends, divorce, and a career-ending car accident.

The mother of two adult daughters, Angie is married to her soul mate, contemporary artist William Haskell. They make their home in the mountains of Santa Fe, New Mexico.